ReBoot Your Relationship

Joe Whitcomb and Savannah Ellis

Published by BEXSI Publishing
www.AuthorYourBrand.com

The opinions expressed by the author are not necessarily those of
Bexsi Publishing, LLC.

This book is designed to provide accurate and authoritative information
with regard to the subject matter covered. This information is given with
the understanding that neither the author nor Bexsi Publishing, LLC is
engaged in rendering legal, professional advice. Since the details of your
situation are fact dependent, you should additionally seek the services of
a competent professional.

ISBN 978-1490942827

Printed in USA by Bexsi Publishing www.AuthorYourBrand.com

TABLE OF CONTENTS

DEDICATION

To my children Sonia, Gannon, Jordanne and Meigan and grand daughter, Skylar

I can never say this or show this enough...I love you! Thank you for loving me all the way through my own humanity and imperfections.

Daddy

To my children Sara, Jacob, & Hannah, my reminders that life is about Love & Relationships .

Savannah Ellis

Introduction

Relationships are complex.

Relationships are, for better or worse, what make us a society, a family and a couple. How we "relate" to other human beings, specifically our significant other, is a barometer for the overall happiness in our lives.

How then, do couples who fall head over heels in love one year come to a place where the manner in which your spouse chews gum makes you contemplate strangulation?

A man's muse can turn into a raving, demanding lunatic, and a woman's knight in shining armor can mystically transform into a belching caveman. How does this happen? On the surface, women are labeled too emotional and men are stereotypically reserved, with no emotional bandwith. Simple, right?

Not so fast.

Part of our challenges is that neither gender deeply understands what the other is truly thinking and feeling. Moreover, there may be a deeper problem, one that may have nothing to do with their relationship at all. The core of most conflicts isn't what "she" did or what "he" said; it is our own personal story; it is interpretation of the circumstance, how we deal with it and how we communicate our internal conflict to our partner. Most arguments start in one area and end up somewhere completely different until neither partner remembers how the discussion started. Until we become aware of our subconscious feelings, develop positive communication styles, and deal with our core issues in a healthy and productive manner, our relationships will continue to stall, wither, and eventually disintegrate.

You can't start working on any meaningful relationship until you work on yourself...thoroughly.

Couples simply do not understand, relate, talk, or listen to one another the way they need to in order to intuitively understand both sides of the conversation. The patterns we use and the *manner* in which we communicate and cope are core elements of why relationships fail. The foundation of a healthy and engaging relationship, be it marriage or otherwise, is simple:

We must authentically connect.

Learning how to authentically connect, communicate, relate and grow is the purpose of this book. We provide a deep overview and examples in this book. However, our experience with thousands of couples have shown a few lacking elements in the journey to restoring relationship. Primarily, couples work best by *experiencing* new shifts in their thinking. Secondly, by using their new tools and technology in an entertaining manner, the process "sticks." We host and facilitate our signature "WE^3 retreats" Using our proprietary WE^3 process. this process helps couples connect to the issues that are the heart of their problems. Together, we remove the obstacles that stand between them. The WE^3 process is experimental, empowering, and entertaining. More information of the WE^3 retreats is given in the Appendix. In the meantime, this book will act as your blueprint to guide you through the rough spots and help you move towards peace, joy and love. You can authentically reconnect with your partner.

You will be able to Reboot Your Relationship.

SAVANNAH ELLIS

Joe and I have taken up the quest to help couples discover what is wrong with their relationships and help them restore the intimate connection they originally had when they first fell in love.

Why it is that after being together for so long, a couple suddenly has major problems? What happened to marital bliss? What happened to "until death do us part?" What happened to the sex?!

First of all, any fall from bliss to blasé is never all that "sudden"; there is always something that has lain buried, perhaps before you even knew one another, or perhaps it was something you thought that was too small to matter at the time. Perhaps what was once insignificant, after years of "sameness," has become huge and infuriating.

Our mission is to "eliminate" the eight-hundred-pound gorilla in the room. We will help you get to the root cause of your discontent, pull it out, analyze it, deal with it, and put it behind you.

Forever.

Background: *When I was getting my undergraduate degree in psychology, I did a lot of work with the Muslim community. In fact, I was married to a Muslim man for ten years. As a white woman from Australia, that singled me out in most Muslim crowds. Nevertheless, I did a lot of work with women and charities back then and became interested in the medical aspect of psychology. My passion was always helping people change their lives, and I've been called upon frequently to do so. For a relationship to not just survive, but thrive, one must be keenly aware of another person's emotional needs, and yes, men have emotional needs just as much as women do. Men just express their emotional needs* differently. In fact, the ten different types of emotional needs (as detailed in chapter one) are equally necessary for both men and women.

A thriving, loving relationship can be boiled down to a single concept. No matter how long a couple has been together, you cannot treat each another like a piece of furniture. When you were courting, whatever you saw in each another was the basis for the **contract** you made for life, the promise of what to expect of each other in your marriage. If ten years down the line one or more of those promises are not being fulfilled, then the relationship is off balance and needs to be corrected. If the courtship is the sales pitch, marriage is the sale, and everything after that is the lifetime warranty.

We'll be reviewing your contract details in this book. The warranty will be yours to uphold.

JOE WHITCOMB

I have had more than twenty years' experience as a relationship coach and therapist, with a focus on helping couples connect and communicate at deeper levels. My battle cry has been, "Connection is why we are here. Life is about relationships. It's what brings purpose and meaning to our lives."

As of 2013, I am a doctoral candidate in marriage and family therapy, but I have already spent a generation helping more than 2,000 couples through their relationship problems. Throughout this experience, I've listened, talked and counseled for decades. However, for rapid, permanent and fun transformational empowerment for couples, nothing has come close to our unique "WE³" system of entertaining, experiential empowerment. In fact, I'm so thrilled to showcase this, I'll share with you my mission. I believe we have the opportunity to not just reboot YOUR relationship, but we can repair the fabric of our nation along the way. Imagine how much better society will function with a million more engaged, empowered couples leading the charge.

It's an audaciously bold goal, but one that stirs my soul.

I formed The Relationship Society to bring experts and couples together to address the epidemic-like loss of social capital in this country and to help couples solve their intimacy and communication problems by promoting the safety-net concept that health is social. Membership into the Relationship Society is free, and I encourage you to join and share with others. http://relationshipsociety.com.

Let me give you a little overview on my philosophy of relationships. Relationships are like a dance. When you're close and in rhythm with one another, the music flows and the dance is effortless. Other times the music you are hearing is not in sync with your partner's melody and you may step on each other's toes. In many cases, the dance of love can turn into a dance of fear and shame. At first you start backing away, then get tentatively closer, back away again, and so on until the music stops and you are just shuffling your feet. Or worse, you leave the dance floor . . . alone.

Your dance of bliss became a dance of dysfunction.

You may be listening to the music, but sometimes you don't hear the melody. Throughout this book, we want to help you hear the music and, as tactfully as I can explain it, get you to become aware that you may be tone deaf.

My goal is to help couples sync their individual melodies and get back into their mutual rhythm again. We'll teach you how to hear the music of your love for one another, go with its flow and teach other new moves in your heart, new songs on your dance floor, and create a romantic ensemble of togetherness.

Just like you had at the beginning. Probably even better.

All relationship problems can be traced to relationship traumas that people have had in their past, one that prevents them from completely bonding with their chosen mate. As Savannah mentioned, when you marry, the relationship is a "contract" and our "warranty" is expected to last for life. Our relationship trauma model is based on the breaking of this contract. It needn't be just about a marriage, but is a breaking of what you thought was significant.

This book is about the philosophy we use in helping individuals and couples deal with the relationship trauma that separates one from the other and helping them become a "We" again. The WE³ system isn't foolproof; you have to practice the dance moves to get it right. But there is one thing I will guarantee: If you actively think, act and interact with an open mind and a grateful heart, you'll be a contender on the next "So You Think You Can Dance" competition for relationships. You'll probably even win.

All relationships are a dance, and we'll teach you the steps.

Cha-cha-cha...

IMPORTANT NOTE:

Throughout this book we will be referring to people as "him" "her" and "they." When you see the word "you," "I," or "we," you may or may not relate your situation to the particular story or example immediately.

Over the years, we have come to realize that information and education changes meaning over time. If a particular example or lesson doesn't makes sense to you immediately, go back and read this book again later. As Jonathan & Sara S. expressed to us during our WE[3] immersion weekends, *"I've heard some of this stuff before, but your positioning of the information made it sound brand new, and by experiencing it, lessons became habits, and habits restored our marriage."*

Chapter One:

WHAT MAKES A RELATIONSHIP GREAT?

"If you want to change the world, love a woman all the way through until she believes you, until her instincts, her visions, her voice, her art, her passion, her wildness has returned to her, until she is a force of love more powerful than all the demons who seek to devalue and destroy her."

-Joe Whitcomb

What makes a relationship great? What should we be looking for? How do we connect with that other person? Many factors create a solid and loving relationship, starting with what each saw in the other upon first meeting, and ending with being compassionate and responsive to the needs of the other person without sacrificing our own needs . . . freedom to love.

This is equally important for both men and women.

A great starting point for healing a damaged relationship is for each person to recall what your spouse saw in *you* when first you met, because that is what he or she is most likely *expecting* you to continue to be. The two of you signed an emotional contract, and it is the breaking of this contract that causes problems in a relationship.

Let's talk about Love.

Of the 17,890,339,443 songs ever written, 99.9 percent of them were about love. Of the 49,003,340 movies ever produced, 94.2 percent of them centered around love. Of the 489,874,843 poems ever written, *all* of them were about love.

NOTE: IT HAS BEEN REPORTED THAT 88 PERCENT
OF ALL STATISTICS ARE MADE UP,
BUT YOU GET THE POINT.

You get the point. Love is not just in our hearts, it's a focal point of our society, culture and life experience. With such a massive amount of culture, thought and focus wouldn't it make sense that there was more of it?

Can I define love?

Nope. Not even close.

Can we discuss love?

Yes…we can even give you a blueprint to it's inner workings.

THE FOUR TYPES OF LOVE

There is a huge difference between how women feel and experience love and how a man feels and experiences it. It's been said that men need sex in order to feel love, and women need to feel loved in order to have sex.

A trite generality, perhaps, but men and women do have

foundational differences and completely opposite ways of feeling and experiencing the emotion of love. Beyond that, there are four different expressions of love; each type must be nurtured for a relationship to continue to be successful. We've broken these down into four basic categories.

The Four Types of Love:

- Friendship
- Passion
- Admiration
- Unconditional

Friendship love. It's not simply the love, but the liking of the other person that creates a bond. Do you like your partner? The liking of a person is not just compiling a "wish list" of attributes, but having a connection that is mutual. You can like someone and not love them and you can love someone and not like them. But, when you like them, it certainly allows for the opportunity for a deeper love. Friendships are trusting. Being vulnerable with another person we trust, makes a person feel safe. Think about your best friend for a moment. Most people can confide with their best friend, because they feel safe being vulnerable with them. When we can be vulnerable AND safe, the connection is strengthened. We gain some degree of strength (when we need it the most) from a connection that allows us to be ourselves. Good friends allow and encourage us to be ourselves. Our best friends like us for a reason. That reason is based in trust.

Passionate love is the type of love that everybody knows; the hot, erotic physical love we feel when we experience a first kiss, a weekend away and the bliss of sexual intercourse. The chemicals released in our body during passionate love are the same ones released when we are high on narcotics.

Being "addicted to love" is not too far off from the truth.

The challenge with relying solely on passionate love as the foundation for a relationship is that passion often masks the subtle quirks, offensive habits or irritating qualities of the person. *"Oh, I don't mind that John smokes that much, he is so good to me!"* or *"Wow, Linda has such a fantastic body! I don't care that she gripes a bit . . . it's worth the hot sex we have."*

It's been said that love is blind. However, it is only passionate, endorphin-based love that causes love blindness. When you move beyond passion, your vision improves.

Admiration love. Mutual respect and friendship are the reasons two people after 30 years of marriage can still get up every morning and feel lucky to have the same person next to them. For example, during a recent WE³ workshop, I was talking about the concept of *love maps* (we'll refer to them later in this book) and the quality of admiring. A friend of mine, Mike, was leaving my seminar early after he finished talking about this concept. Being a professional golfer, I assumed he was heading for the golf course. But when I asked him where he was going, and he said, *"I am attending my wife's art exhibition."*

"Oh, really?" I said.

I asked Mike if he loved art, and he said, *"No, I actually hate art, but I love to watch my wife's face light up and her body come alive when she's living out of her passion. When she comes to life like that, it totally turns me on!"*

Did this man love his wife? Of course. By attending a boring art exhibition in order to see her bask in joy was a clear statement of love on a higher level.

In order to start, develop, grow, and thrive in any relationship, all four love styles need to be understood, embraced and practiced.

Imagine if you are clicking on an icon on your computer, and your computer isn't working the way it should. Many relationships are treated like broken computers. We trade them in for a new model.

However, our files and history are on that computer. We always bring those along with us. While the shiny, new computer looks tempting, it ia easier to simply upgrade your operating system, instead of discarding the entire computer.

The same is true of your relationship.

When you simply upgrade your operating system, you get to keep all your files, but the manner in which you operate improves.

Unconditional love. Unconditional love is based on commitment and action. When love is based on these qualities, nearly any storm is weathered and an individual's values are shared equally. When both people have unconditional love in their hearts and in their character, they still have challenges, of course, but quitting is never an option. The value of commitment is placed above and beyond the passion (or lack thereof).

Unconditional love is more than commitment. Unconditional love is based on a love with no conditions. The love itself is revered. The person is respected, but if their love were an entity, it would be placed ahead of the person. Unconditional love leads naturally to connection for connection's sake and admiration. In fact, when you love someone unconditionally, it means you accept their faults and defects. Unconditional love does not dismiss passionate love, nor are we placing these four styles in any type of hierarchy. Each one must be understood and practiced.

BONUS: Beyond unconditional love, there is Wabi Sabi love. Wabi-Sabi is an ancient principle of Japanese culture that involves honoring the imperfections of the other person. In Japan, if a treasured vase is cracked, instead of throwing it away, the vase is placed on a pedestal, in a museum and a light is focused on the crack! In some cases they would even inlay 24-carat gold into the crack to accentuate and honor it. Instead of replacing the vase, as is common in many cultures, the Japanese honor the imperfection.

We all have imperfections and cracks. Instead of ignoring, showing contempt, or hiding the imperfection, it is held up and honored. We teach couples at our WE^3 retreats to go from annoyed to enjoyed by learning to honor each other's imperfections. While it sounds awkward at first, once you acknowledge your own imperfections, it doesn't take long to embrace a fresh and revered perspective with your partner's imperfections.

Once you master your basic loves styles, you will be able to reboot your relationship as easily as you reboot your computer and be open to each other regardless of any relationship-style computer crashes. It is only through the combination of the four styles that long-lasting love and a highly connected relationship can thrive.

How do we get there? Our WE^3 experiential programs give you all of the strategies and tools to thrive in your relationship, regardless of the depths of dysfunction it may be in. We'll cover the complete process throughout this book. Those who qualify may be invited to experience a life-changing weekend at one of our exclusive resort retreats. As a precursor to the WE^3 system, let us discuss two elements that are critical to the path: *vulnerability* and *trust.*

Prior to embracing deep and long-lasting romance, the components of trust and vulnerability are two of the things that bring people together and create the recipe for love.

WHAT MAKES PEOPLE FALL IN LOVE

What is the difference between two people who fall madly in love and two people who are just friends? Beyond the obvious qualities of physical attraction and mutual chemistry, what creates the deepest emotional intimacy is the level of courage it takes to be completely vulnerable with the other person.

Yikes!

Men, being vulnerable is about as appealing as a nail in the foot. Ladies, you know all too well how fragile you are when vulnerable. For either gender, displaying your imperfections for potential ridicule and revealing your authentic emotions for someone else requires courage and trust. Your fears, pains, dreams, and passions are on display in a way you would never *dare* to share without being confident that sharing those vulnerabilities won't be exploited.

Some people have described love as a form of courage. Certainly, bearing your soul requires an amount of courage. When you are willing to get past the ambiguities of life and say, "I love you," you have taken the first step onto the dance floor of being vulnerable.

What makes people fall in love? What are the mechanisms of this dance?

Vulnerability

As a general rule, women are more comfortable being vulnerable than men. Boys are taught not to cry, and girls are conditioned to communicate emotionally.

This isn't just psychological fluff; there is actual neuroscience behind it. When testosterone enters the womb as a baby is being formed, it will split a boy's brain right to left, leaving more of a compartmentalization between their logical and emotional centers. Women, on the other hand, have a stronger connection between the logical brain and their emotional brain. This leaves women with a need to connect emotionally. Consequently, they also retain a fear of disconnection. Men, on the other hand, tend to be more shame-based and rein in their emotions more readily than women.

When a man gets introduced to a problem or something negative, they normally feel a deep seated urge to "fix it." If they cannot, their masculinity is challeged and they feel imperfect, defective, and lacking in control. A woman, on the other hand, has a need to open up to another, share for the sake of sharing and connection. When it comes to a relationship, a man who understands this need will not only allow her to open up to him but, when he feels safe, will open up to her as well. This mutual vulnerability and trust always creates a bond.

The vulnerability/trust bond need not be escalated to love, of course. Friendships, business relationships and child/parent relationships are all based on a foundation of trust and vulnerability. While varying degrees of trust and vulnerability may not affect a non-romantic relationship, for a romantically involved couple, however, the ability to be vulnerable and trust is paramount to growing that relationship into a solid union.

Trust

Trust is foundational from birth. It becomes internalized very early around the secure attachments we form as infants. When we have such secure attachments, we can securely connect with others.

Research with infants has show us the building blocks of attachments and trust in the brain. MRI brain scans have mapped an infant's experience of trust when there is comfort, trust and proximity to the mother.

Reactive attachment disorders, where babies are abandoned or rejected, show quite a different scan. The scans display a pattern of large black spots on the brain map; these correspond gaps create a hard-wired difficulty with trust and their ability to create attachments. If our brains were simply computers, these black spots would be significant glitches in the programming.

Trust is our safety net. *"Will you trust me if I fall?" "Can I be 100% open and honest with you without getting hurt?"* Neuroscientists have discovered that the human brain is a social brain that constantly searches for safety, comfort, and connection. When those qualities are present and experienced, trust follows naturally.

How trust is engendered differs between a man and a woman. Women normally look for 5 foundational factors:

- Security
- Safety
- Stability
- Empathy
- Acceptance

Men, on the other hand, trust for a woman who:

- Listens

- Is Compassionate
- Connects with him physically
- Validates him
- Respects him, his masculinity, and his ability to provide.

Mutual trust is reached with these two viewpoints converge. A woman will respect a man when he fulfills her needs. In turn, that respect makes the man more prone to trust her and provide more of her needs. Trust is similar to two magnets; properly aligned they will pull each other closer with ever-increasing force, but face them the wrong way in and they will continue to repel.

Connecting: What Each Wants

Generally speaking, men and women want something different from the other. Women want face-to-face communication, an intimate connection. Men, on the other hand, often want a playmate, someone to be there in their adventures and other activities. He needs a companion and a cheerleader.

When there is gender-based conflict, men are far more likely to emotionally stonewall the relationship. A man's silence is often perceived as rejection. Rejection creates disconnection. Disconnection creates more fear. Fear causes more complaints. More complaints create more withdraw.

The vicious cycle spirals down.

The silence-rejection-disconnection-fear-complaint-silence cycle is similar to a computer program stuck in a logic loop. The relationship sits there like a computer -- doing nothing but eating up memory and computer resources until you get fed up and power it off.

A good connection is formed by equal amounts of love and

respect. She needs love, connection, and belonging, he needs respect, significance, and to feel needed by her. The first step to interrupt the downward spiral is to recognize it. Once recognized, you can reboot your love machine.

Chemistry Of Love

The physical chemistry behind love is also called limerence. Limerence can be explained chemically by oxytocin being released with touching, cuddling and sexual contact. Research shows this results in the "reward" part of the brain lighting up as it's being flushed with dopamine. Couples in limerence can continue to feel the effects from 12 months to 2 years. Once the limerance dissapates, many people fall "out" of love. Serial daters and short marriages are often victims of this limited type of love.

In order to build a meaningful relationship past this endorphin-induced love, couples must build strong commitments, emotional connections, and an effective manner to resolve conflicts. Limerence isn't necessarily a shallow or insignificant type of love, but limerence without the other types of love won't be strong enough to support a long-term relationship.

If your limerence fire has flickered or smoldered out, here is a quick 5-step pattern to rekindle that spark.

1. Think back to when the love came from a place of *desire* and not a place of demand.
2. Recall clear experiences in your past and relive them in your mind in as much detail as possible.
3. Physicallly go back to any location where limerence was shining and anchor your mind to that time/place.

4. Use all of your senses to rekindle those memories and create a new, loving and intimate experience while recalling your past limerence.

5. Capture your new memories on camera and be 100% present in the moment so you can recall your new experience in as much detail as possible in the future.

Closeness

Closeness is both physical and emotional. Sometimes, a good cure for fading limerence can be a simple touch. Often, a physical reassurance will fight off the uncertainty and anxiety of disconnection. The same example can be said for emotional closeness. Reaching out and "touching" your partner emotionally on a consistent basis will do wonders for your connection.

For example, suppose circumstances occur and you don't communicate for a day or more. If this is out of the normal closeness your partner is accustomed to, you may get a, *"Why didn't you call me?"* This isn't a battle for dominance or blame, it is a fight for connection.

In order to remain close, get closer. In order to connect fully, keep connecting.

Playfulness

To connect without words, experience each through playful experiences. You put your cold feet against your wife's legs in bed at night and she's laughing telling you to *"Stop that!"* It's light fun, connecting through humor, and allows defense mechanisms to melt away.

Men in particularly tend to connect more through play and

sports, just as they did as boys. If a woman leaves a message, *"We need to talk"* in man's mind, that is code for *"I'm in trouble."* He may instantly withdraw behind his emotional barriers. Instead of drawing a line in the sand, pick up a frisbee, head outside and ask some questions. All of us are more likely to chat when sensitive subjects are discussed in an open and non-confrontational manner. Play. Laugh. Have fun.

Sexuality

Ah…sex. The main event. After a couple gets over the awkwardness of learning what makes the other's motor run, sex is certainly one of the more exciting areas of intimate relationships.

Relationships based on sex can also disintegrate quickly when it fails. Most successful relationships also have good sexual compatibility. Sexual intimacy keeps the oxytocin pumping. As we've discussed, however, limerence, by its very nature, does not improve with age. Add a few children, career challenges, and "father time" to the equation and you'll understand that sexual desire and sexual connection is never constant.

Sex without love is never a good long-term plan. Sex with increased emotional intimacy raises a couples connection and bond. In order to raise the bar sexually, couples should explore their mutually vulnerable areas. Sexual vulnerability is not much different than emotional vulnerability and it's cousin-trust. Sexual connection increases with increased vulnerability and trust.

While all human beings require an amount of certainty, we also need, to varying degrees, an amount of uncertainty. For many women, the desire for certainty is larger than uncertainty.

In the bedroom, a woman definitely needs to feel safe and secure in order to open up to a man. While a man's masculine tendency of adventure and uncertainty is generally higher, he must be aware of the feminine requirement for safety (certainty) before leading her into the adventure of uncertainty.

Sexually, knowing how to make each other orgasm is one of the first milestones of an intimate relationship. However, being able to flip that switch with a new dance is what makes the oxytocin flow. If you don't change things up and continue to play the same tune over and over again, sex becomes a tradition, an act and even a chore instead of a thrilling dance of discovery, intimacy and the ultimate dance of closeness.

Balance each other's needs for certainty and uncertainty. It's fine to employ your favorite position because you know it works, but it's equally playful and exciting to try the "Padlock" Kama Sutra position and see what happens!

You may be experiencing some or all 7 elements of love. Regardless of where you are in your relationship journey, keep all 7 in mind as you explore, build and strengthen your relationships.

- Vulnerability
- Trust
- Connecting: What Each Wants
- Chemistry of Love
- Closeness
- Playfulness
- Sexuality

Creating strong and healthy relationships, like your computer, require anti-virus software, cleaning and maintenance. Neglecting your relationship is as good as destroying it. Let's dig a little deeper into what makes a good relationship great.

What Makes A Great Relationship

There are thousands of studies and reports on the elements of great relationships and marriages. The similarities between many of these studies have shown people in a great relationships have completed a number of psychological "tasks." Here is a summary:

- **Separate emotionally from the family you grew up in:** Not to the point of estrangement, but enough so that your identity is separate from that of your parents and siblings. After all, you should be closer to your spouse than you ever could or should be to any other member of your family.

- **Build togetherness based on a shared intimacy and identity, while at the same time set boundaries to protect each partner's autonomy:** A couple should almost be as one, a single unit, but at the same time one is not a clone of the other.

- **Establish a rich and pleasurable sexual relationship and protect it from the intrusions of the workplace and family obligations:** That connection you have with one another is part emotional and part physical; one failing will affect the other and thence the couple as a whole. Keep it safe in its own special place. When having that intimate encounter, make sure no distractions from home or work will intrude. After all, if you decide to cut it short because the boss called with something "urgent" that really could have waited an extra hour, whom do you think your wife is going to blame; the boss or you?

- **For couples with children, embrace the daunting roles of parenthood and absorb the impact of a baby's entrance into the marriage:** Parenthood should not be considered an inconvenience intruding into your relationship, but rather a physical manifestation of the love the two of you share for one another. Every time you look at that baby, you should be reminded of the one who helped you make it.

- **Learn to continue the work of protecting the privacy of you and your spouse as a couple:** What goes on between you and your partner, for good and for bad, is really no on else's business but your own. Others need to respect that boundary and keep their meddling noses out, including parents. Many a good marriage has been ruined by the well-intentioned interference of in-laws.

- **Confront and master the inevitable crises of life:** As the saying goes (to paraphrase), stuff happens. The trick is not to run from the problems that arise, but to confront and solve these problems... together.

- **Maintain the strength of the marital bond in the face of adversity:** No matter what, that bond the two of you share should be the strongest thing in your Universe. Your home could be flooded, your kids near death, and your dog run over by a train, but you should still be there for one another even in the worst of it all. A house divided cannot stand, and neither can a couple divided.

- **The marriage should be a safe haven in which partners are able to express their differences, anger and conflict:** A good marriage is one in which both people feel they can express any grievances they have against one another, discuss and argue them through to resolution, and yet know that they will still be there for one another, still love each other, after all is said and done. It's like the old comic scene in which a couple is arguing rather loudly, someone else comes in to intrude with his two cents worth, then as one the couple turns and shouts at the poor guy, "Shut up, we're arguing!" It should be that safe.

- **Use humor and laughter to keep things in perspective and to avoid boredom and isolation:** Humor is the cure for all ills. It's a great means of bringing people together, of allowing you to see a problem for the very minor obstacle that it is, and for reminding people why they got together in the first place.

- **Nurture and comfort each other, satisfying each partner's needs for dependency and offering continuing encouragement and support:** Would not your right hand tenderly nurse your left hand when it is cut? You are more than simply two separate people, but this needs to be constantly demonstrated, one to the other. Be there for your mate's hurts and doubts, but also for their joys and dreams, as the other will in turn be here for yours.

- **Keep alive the early romantic, idealized images of falling in love, while facing the sober realities of the changes wrought by time:** How many times have you seen news reports of old couples married some sixty years and seen that they still have the look of doe-eyed teenagers in their eyes for one another? Enough times to get the point?

THE 10 TYPES OF EMOTIONAL NEEDS

There are 10 different types of emotional needs that both people in a relationship need to have satisfied; ten different emotional levels on which they need to connect. Each has its own importance, and they must all be kept in balance to maintain a good relationship.

- ➢ *Affection:* Something as simple as brushing up against one another as you pass by, showing affection without anything sexual involved. Believe it or not, guys want it as much as the women.

- ➢ *Sexual fulfillment:* The physical act, with or without the above stated affection. There is an old saying that "women need to feel loved in order to have sex while men need sex in order to feel loved." A corollary might go something like "if a woman uses sex as a tool for her husband, she should not be surprised to find him being unfaithful."

- ➢ *Conversation:* Communication is a dynamic process of discovery and connection that energizes one another.

- ➢ *Recreational needs and companionship:* People don't spend enough time playing and laughing together.

- ➢ *Honesty and openness*: Builds trust in a relationship.

- ➢ *Physical attractiveness:* A huge issue for men and women alike and probably a book in itself.

- ➢ *Financially supporting each other:* Most fights between couples begin and end over financial issues.

- ➢ *Domestic support:* What does each partner do in the home?

- ➢ *Family commitment.* How committed are you to family issues and chores around the house?

- ➢ *Admiration:* Everyone craves admiration for what they do, so can you expect any less from your spouse?

Affection is particularly important for men in the long run.

When a woman forgets to be affectionate this can push a man away to the point where he gets his needs met elsewhere. Affection can be tied up with sex, but needn't be. Affection can be as simple as an opening a car door or an extra squeeze of the hand. Affection is the little things you do and say for one another that let the other know that you care.

How often do you show little signs of affection? Details matter in any endeavor, and when it comes to relationships, *Affection* is a detail that matters. You can attract more flies with honey than vinegar, or in this case you can attract more feelings of love and bonding with affection that non-affection. Be the honey; show your partner a moment or two of passing unplanned affection. An unusually long stare or authentic smile can go a long way.

Sexual fulfillment is an often talked about subject for many couples. The chemical, biological and emotional requirement for sex in a healthy relationship shouldn't be ignored. In healthy relationships, couples have sex about three to four times a week. When you married one another, part of the promise was to be there for each other physically, to be each other's sexual partner; the vow did not say, "Once a month on Sundays." If you cannot find the time, or if you let the dog sleep between the both of you, (unless there is a medical problem) you are avoiding the issue. This is the love of your life, the one to whom you have unconditionally sworn, and it is worth your time to do whatever it takes to reconnect emotionally and sexually.

Many people surround themselves with the drama of sex, fear of the truth about sex, fear of the rejection of not having sex, and never address the direct question, which is, "Why are you not having sex?" What is the issue behind it? Maybe your sexual role model set a bad example. Maybe the wife feels ignored or not respected and doesn't have the sex drive, or maybe he's not showering and she simply doesn't want to touch him.

From Savannah:

"I had a client that was a wealthy farmer. He felt like he didn't have to put in all that much effort and would often wear the same pants every day and not shower because he was just going out early the next morning to get dirty again. His wife, on the other hand, was repulsed and didn't want to touch him. This was her husband and it felt awkward that she should have to tell him to take a shower. It took her months before the three of us were able to simple put hygiene on the table."

It's not unusual to be reluctant about talking about sexual problems. With most couples, there is quite a bit of emotion attached to it. People can get defensive regardless of the issue. "In the case of the farmer who needed a shower, his wife simply invited him into her shower. Without telling him he smelled, she was able to reset some habits and focus on their intimacy instead of hygiene."

Conversation is something we can have with anybody every day, so why converse less with your spouse? The level and amount of conversation you have with him or her needs to be such that your partner feels validated and important. With mutual trust and friendship, share openly and fully. A lack of trust creates inauthentic conversations. Many married couples fall into "How was work, today?" or "What time is the school board meeting?" conversations. While these may be important to make sure Timmy gets to soccer practice on time, be sure to also check in with each other's hearts, as well.

Expressing an interest in what the other person is saying

makes that person feel validated. If you stop talking, if you feel there is no need to "have that same conversation again", or start limiting your statements to factual and procedural matters, the need for conversational connection may be met elsewhere. Many emotional affairs are seeded in the monotony of task-based conversations between couples.

Conversation is not the same as nagging, or the wife pouncing on the husband the minute he gets home. Allow each other the space and time to decompress and check in on the basics before digging deep into each other's hearts and souls. Being heard and knowing how to listen is the heart of conversation. Good conversation is the beginnings of connection.

Recreational companionship. Successful couples spend 10 to 15 hours per week of quality time together to affirm a happy and long lasting relationship. You probably spent a good deal of quality companionship time together when you were courting, so keep couring. After all, that was the reason for the courtship in the first place: to spend time together, not just spend twenty years paying off a mortgage.

What did you do when you were dating? Was it a walk in the ing league, or biking along a mountain trail. Simple or involved, at home or on a trip, be creative and spontaneous.

Just because you got married, does **not** mean you have to stop courting one another. The opposite is true. Successful couples continue to date each other while they are married.

Physical Attractiveness can be a significant emotional need for many couples, and many people are uncomfortable talking about this value with our spouse. In our 20's and 30's it is often accepted that we look good and stay in shape. As a couple enter their midlife, two distinct paths tend to emerge. Some people accept the effects of gravity as a normal consequence of aging. Other's go on a health kick, join a gym and refuse to "age gracefully." If one spouse fights for this value and the other does not, the disconnect of physical attractiveness can quitely chip away at our other secure connections.

I had one client that stopped kissing her husband ten years prior. When I asked her why, she said, "He's a bad kisser. I never mentioned that to him, but it didn't seem to impact our relationship."

For the wife, this was not a high value. However, this lack of affection affected his emotional need for physical attractiveness and her avoidance of the issue accelerated the disconnect.

Honesty is the glue that holds all the other values together. Without honesty, being attractive, openness and all the other values reside on a house of cards. When we embrace trust (being vulnerable without fear of disconnect) we can be honest. Honesty, without tact, of course doesn't build any emotional bridges. Be sensitive to his or her feelings and how you deliver your honest feelings. In the above kissing example, telling someone their faults accentuates the negative. It would be better to encourage a positive behavior, such as saying, "Honey, whatever happened to those passionate lip locks you used to give me?" and say it with a smile and a hug. Fulfill your mutual needs for honesty in a postive, playful manner.

Financial Security directly relates to emotions. Your emotional state governs everything you do, including investing, impulse buying and budgeting. Communication and values regarding money can make or break a lot a couple. When both people have similar values regarding money, financial security is a natural, emotional dividend.

When there are two separate spending and saving patterns with a couple, disagreements are most definitely assured. In many cases, the value we put on money only scratches the surface of how we relate and embrace each other's core beliefs. Are you opening up, connecting and trusting your spouse if you withhold the sharing of finances? A common definittion of marriage is two who become one, connecting completely with the other, and trusting one another enough to get past the, "This stuff over here is mine and that stuff over there is yours." Sharing financials and trusting your partner to appreciate your beliefs does more than balances a checkbook. It will balance your faith in each other.

From Joe:

"I was working with a couple in their 60's. During the husband's entire life he was the breadwinner, while she had been the housewife. They were nearing retirement when the sparks of discontent began to fly. He had worked fourteen-hour days as a security guard, but when he came home at the end of the day, instead of letting him relax she would began to nag him about what else he was not doing. He would then complain that she had not only never worked a day in her life but also made it quite clear that she never wanted to work or contribute financially. He felt that if she was able to contribute and understand what it was like to actually earn some money and give back to the family rather than just taking, he would feel more validated and loved. Even if she volunteered, it would have allowed her to talk a walk in his

shoes."

Financial planning, beliefs about money, saving and lifestyle are items best talked about *before* you get married. Discussing how things will be handled, and what sort of financial input is to be expected from each person will ease any false expectations for the future.

Domestic Support and *Family Commitment* are key emotional elements that require thorough understanding by both parties, regardless of who handles most of the tasks. In many traditional home dynamics, domestic chores fall to the woman. If this is true in your household, how does the husband support her in the day-to-day chores? Is she always taking out the trash and cleaning up while he sits in front of the television exhausted from his full day? Are both parents equally helping with homework for the children?

Regardless of who is leading and tackling these responsibilities, both domestic support and family commitments require constant acknowledgment and awareness in order to feed the emotional bond you both need as a team.

Many a fight has started over something as silly as taking out the trash or fixing a faucet. Are these tiny items worth jepoardizing your domestic contract? If either of you feel overwhelmed, count to 10 and instead of lashing out at each other, take a step back and look at the situation from the other person's perspective. If you've been at work all day, you may need a little down time to decompress before helping with dinner or assisting with homework. If you've been couped up all day and desperate for adult conversation, allow a brief buffer zone of time to elapse before launching into a stream of tasks, requests or conversation.

For couples who don't work together, be keenly aware that the other person is most likely busting their hump domestically, economically (or both!) to make your house a home. Give each other the space, acknowledgement and affirmations they deserve and need.

And finally, *Admiration*. When has the need to be admired by a loved one *not* been an emotional issue? No one wants to be ignored, especially by his or her significant other. They want to be admired for what and who they are, men in particular. When you stop showing admiration for your spouse, he or she will begin to feel like they aren't loved or needed, and that can lead to growing farther and farther apart. Men need to be affirmed as men…to be acknowledged for their masculine qualities, regardless of their profession. It is the smart spouse who encourages and admires her man. Likewise, no woman has ever rejected a sincere compliment. Even if she doesn't respond externally, internally, every woman wants to be admired and revered as the beautiful princess you once told her she was.

A relationship is an emotional contract, and marriage shares many of the same qualities as a business deal (exchanging value with another party). You need to collaborate with one another and achieve common emotional ground. The goal, after all, is for you *both* to be winners. Once you realize that, then you are on the road to having not just a good relationship, but a great relationship.

Below is a great worksheet you can use to continuously monitor your mutual emotional needs. Make copies of this and share your progress openly and without judgement.

1. Affection (the expression of love in words, cards, gifts, hugs, kisses, and courtesies; creating an environment that clearly and repeatedly expresses love)

A. Need for affection: Indicate how much you need affection by circling the appropriate number:

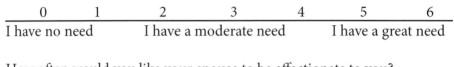

0	1	2	3	4	5	6
I have no need		I have a moderate need			I have a great need	

How often would you like your spouse to be affectionate to you?
_____ times each day/week/month (circle one).

If you are not shown affection by your spouse as often as you indicated above, how does it make yo
B. Evaluation of spouse's affection: Indicate your satisfaction with your spouse's affection toward you by circling the appropriate number.

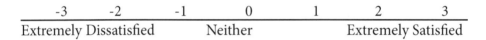

-3	-2	-1	0	1	2	3
Extremely Dissatisfied			Neither		Extremely Satisfied	

My spouse gives me (circle the appropriate letter)
a. all the affection I need, and I like the way he/she does it.
b. not enough affection, but when he/she does it, it is the way I like it.
c. all the affection I need, but it is not the way I like it.
d. not enough affection, and when he/she tries, it is not the way I like it.

Explain how your need for affection could be better satisfied in your marriage.

2. Sexual Fulfillment (a sexual experience that brings out a predictably enjoyable sexual response in both of you that is frequent enough for both of you).

A. Need for sexual fulfillment: Indicate how much you need sexual fulfillment by circling the appropriate number.

0	1	2	3	4	5	6
I have no need		I have a moderate need			I have a great need	

How often would you like your spouse to engage in sexual relations with you? _____ times each day/week/month (circle one).

If your spouse does not engage in sexual relations with you as often as you indicated above, how does it make you feel (circle the appropriate letter)?
a. Very unhappy.
b. Neither happy nor unhappy.
c. Somewhat unhappy
d. Happy not to engage in sex.

B. Evaluation of sexual relations with your spouse: Indicate your satisfaction with your spouse's sexual relations with you by circling the appropriate number.

-3	-2	-1	0	1	2	3
Extremely Dissatisfied			Neither		Extremely Satisfied	

My spouse gives me (circle the appropriate letter)
a. all the sex I need, and I like the way he/she does it.
b. not enough sex, but when he/she does it, it is the way I like it.
c. all the sex I need, but it is not the way I like it.
d. not enough sex, and when we do have sex it is not the way I like it

Explain how your need for sexual fulfillment could be better satisfied in your marriage.

3. Conversation (talking about events of the day, personal feelings, and plans for the future; showing interest in your favorite topics of conversation; balancing conversation; using it to inform, investigate, and understand you; and giving you undivided attention)

A. Need for conversation: Indicate how much you need conversation by circling the appropriate number:

0	1	2	3	4	5	6
I have no need			I have a moderate need			I have a great need

How often would you like your spouse to talk with you?
_____ times each day/week/month (circle one).

If your spouse does not talk with you as often as you indicated above, how does it make you feel (circle the appropriate letter)?
a. Very unhappy.
b. Somewhat unhappy.
c. Neither happy nor unhappy
d. Happy not to talk with my spouse.

B. Evaluation of conversation with your spouse: Indicate your satisfaction with your spouse's conversation with you by circling the appropriate number.

-3	-2	-1	0	1	2	3
Extremely Dissatisfied			Neither			Extremely Satisfied

My spouse gives me (circle the appropriate letter)
a. all the conversation I need, and I like the way he/she does it.
b. not enough conversation, but when he/she does it, it is the way I like it.
c. all the conversation I need, but it is not the way I like it.
d. not enough conversation and when we do it is not the way I like it

Explain how your need for conversation could be better satisfied in your marriage.

4. Recreational Companionship (developing interest in your favorite recreational activities, learning to be proficient in them, and joining you in those activities).

A. Need for recreational companionship: Indicate how much yo u need recreational companionship by circling the appropriate number:

0	1	2	3	4	5	6
I have no need		I have a moderate need			I have a great need	

How often would you like your spouse join you in recreational activities? _____ times each day/week/month (circle one).

If your spouse does not join you in recreational activities as often as you indicated above, how does it make you feel (circle the appropriate letter)?
a. Very unhappy
b. Somewhat unhappy
c. Neither happy nor unhappy
d. Happy not to join spouse in recreation.

B. Evaluation of recreational companionship with your spouse: Indicate your satisfaction with your spouse's recreational companionship with you by circling the appropriate number.

-3	-2	-1	0	1	2	3
Extremely Dissatisfied			Neither		Extremely Satisfied	

My spouse gives me (circle the appropriate letter)
a. all the recreational companionship I need, and I like the way he/she does it.
b. not enough recreational companionship, but when he/she does it, it is the way I like it.
c. all the recreational companionship I need, but it is not the way I like it.
d. not enough recreational companionship, and when he/she tries, it is not the way I like it.

Explain how your need for recreational companionship could be better satisfied in your marriage.

5. Honesty and Openness (revealing positive and negative feelings, events of the past, daily events and schedule, plans for the future; not leaving a false impression; answering questions truthfully and completely).

A. Need for honesty and openness: Indicate how much you need honesty by circling the appropriate number:

0	1	2	3	4	5	6
I have no need		I have a moderate need			I have a great need	

Which of the following areas of honesty and openness would you like from your spouse (circle the letter(s) that apply to you)?
a. Sharing positive and negative emotional reactions to significant aspects of life.
b. Sharing information regarding his/her personal history.
c. Sharing information about his/her daily activities.
d. Sharing information about his/her future schedule and plans.

If your spouse fails to be open and honest in those areas that you indicated above, how does it make you feel (circle appropriate letter)?
a. Very unhappy
b. Somewhat unhappy
c. Neither happy nor unhappy
d. Happy not to have honesty and openness.

B. Evaluation of spouse's honesty and openness: Indicate your satisfaction with your spouse's honesty and openness with you by circling the appropriate number.

-3	-2	-1	0	1	2	3
Extremely Dissatisfied			Neither		Extremely Satisfied	

My spouse is (circle the appropriate letter)
a. honest and open with me, and I like the way he/she does it.

b. not honest and open enough with me, but when he/she does it, it is the way I like it.
c. honest and open with me, but it is not the way I like it.
d. not honest and open with me, and when he/she tries, it is not the way I like it.

Explain how your need for honesty & openness could be better satisfied in your marriage.

6. An Attractive Spouse (keeping physically fit with diet and exercise, wearing hair and clothing in a way that you find attractive and tasteful).

A. Need for an attractive spouse: Indicate how much you need an attractive spouse by circling the appropriate number:

0	1	2	3	4	5	6
I have no need		I have a moderate need			I have a great need	

Which of the following characteristics of attractiveness mean the most to you (circle the letter(s) that apply to you)?
a. Physical fitness and normal weight.
b. Attractive choice of clothes.
c. Attractive hairstyle.
d. Good physical hygiene.
e. Attractive facial makeup.
f. Other _____

If your spouse does not have those characteristics that you circled above, how does it make you feel (circle the appropriate letter)?
a. Very unhappy.
b. Somewhat unhappy
c. Neither happy nor unhappy
d. Happy not to have an attractive spouse.

B. Evaluation of spouse's attractiveness: Indicate your satisfaction with your spouse's attractiveness by circling the appropriate number.

-3	-2	-1	0	1	2	3
Extremely Dissatisfied			Neither		Extremely Satisfied	

My spouse is (circle the appropriate letter)
a. attractive to me, and I like the way he/she does it.
b. not attractive to me, but when he/she was, I like the way he/she achieved it.

c. attractive to me, but I do not like the way he/she achieves it.
d. not attractive to me, and when he/she was, I did not like the way it was achieved.

Explain how your need for an attractive spouse could be better satisfied in your marriage.

7. Financial Support (the provision of financial resources to house, feed, and clothe your family at a standard of living acceptable to you, but avoiding travel and working hours that are unacceptable)

A. Need for financial support: Indicate how much you need financial support by circling the appropriate number:

0	1	2	3	4	5	6
I have no need		I have a moderate need			I have a great need	

How much money would you like your spouse to earn to support you (and your children)? _____

If your spouse does not earn the amount you indicated above, how does it make you feel (circle the appropriate letter)?
a. Very unhappy.
b. Somewhat unhappy.
c. Neither happy nor unhappy.
d. Happy not to have my spouse provide support.

B. Evaluation of spouse's financial support: Indicate your satisfaction with your spouse's financial support of you by circling the appropriate number.

-3	-2	-1	0	1	2	3
Extremely Dissatisfied			Neither		Extremely Satisfied	

My spouse (circle the appropriate letter)
a. earns enough money to support me, and I like the way he/she earns it.
b. does not earn enough to support me, but I like the way he/she earns it.
c. earns enough money to support me, but I do not like the way he/she earns it.
d. does not enough to support me, and I do not like the way he/she earns it.

Explain how your need for financial support could be better satisfied in your marriage.

8. Domestic Support (creation of a home environment for you that offers a refuge from the stresses of life; management of the home and care of the children—if any are at home— including but not limited to cooking meals, washing dishes, washing and ironing clothes, housecleaning).

A. Need for domestic support: Indicate how much you need domestic support by circling the appropriate number:

0	1	2	3	4	5	6
I have no need		I have a moderate need			I have a great need	

How much time would you like your spouse to be engaged in domestic support?
_____ hours each day/week/month (circle one).

If your spouse does not spend as much time engaged in domestic support as you indicated above, how does it make you feel (circle the appropriate letter)?
a. Very unhappy.
b. Somewhat unhappy.
c. Neither happy nor unhappy.
d. Happy not to have domestic support.

B. Evaluation of spouse's domestic support: Indicate your satisfaction with your spouse's domestic support by circling the appropriate number.

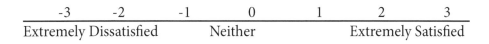

-3	-2	-1	0	1	2	3
Extremely Dissatisfied			Neither		Extremely Satisfied	

My spouse gives me (circle the appropriate letter)
a. all the domestic support I need, and I like the way he/she does it.
b. not enough domestic support, but when he/she does it, it is the way I like it.
c. all the domestic support I need, but it is not the way I like it.

d. not enough domestic support, and when he/she tries, it is not the way I like it.

Explain how your need for domestic support could be better satisfied in your marriage.

9. Family Commitment (scheduling sufficient time and energy for the moral and educational development of your children; reading to them, taking them on frequent outings, developing the skill in appropriate child-training methods and discussing those methods with you; avoiding any child-training methods or disciplinary action that does not have your enthusiastic support).

A. Need for family commitment: Indicate how much you need family commitment by circling the appropriate number:

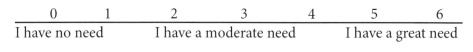

0	1	2	3	4	5	6
I have no need		I have a moderate need			I have a great need	

How much time would you like your spouse to be engaged in family commitment?

_____ hours each day/week/month (circle one).

If your spouse does not spend as much time engaged in family commitment as you indicated above, how does it make you feel (circle the appropriate letter)?
a. Very unhappy.
b. Somewhat unhappy
c. Neither happy nor unhappy
d. Happy not to have family commitment.

B. Evaluation of spouse's family commitment: Indicate your satisfaction with your spouse's family commitment by circling the appropriate number.

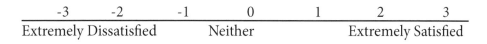

-3	-2	-1	0	1	2	3
Extremely Dissatisfied			Neither		Extremely Satisfied	

My spouse (circle the appropriate letter)
a. commits enough time to the family and spends it in ways I like

b. does not commit enough time to the family, but when he/she does it, it's spent in ways that I like.
c. commits enough time to the family, but does not spend it in ways that I like.
d. does not commit enough time to the family, and when he/she does, it is not spent in ways that I like it.

Explain how your need for family commitment could be better satisfied in your marriage.

10. Admiration (respecting, valuing, and appreciating you clearly and often).

A. Need for admiration: Indicate how much you need admiration by circling the appropriate number:

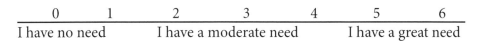

0	1	2	3	4	5	6
I have no need		I have a moderate need			I have a great need	

How often would you like your spouse to admire you?
_____ times each day/week/month (circle one).

If your spouse does not admire you as often as you indicated above, how does it make you feel (circle the appropriate letter)?
a. Very unhappy.
b. Somewhat unhappy.
c. Neither happy nor unhappy.
d. Happy not to be admired.

B. Evaluation of spouse's admiration: Indicate your satisfaction with your spouse's admiration toward you by circling the appropriate number.

-3	-2	-1	0	1	2	3
Extremely Dissatisfied			Neither		Extremely Satisfied	

My spouse gives me (circle the appropriate letter)
a. all the admiration I need, and I like the way he/she does it.
b. not enough admiration, but when he/she does it, it is the way I like it.
c. all the admiration I need, but it is not the way I like it.
d. not enough admiration, and when he/she tries, it is not the way I like it.

Explain how your need for admiration could be better satisfied in your marriage.

Chapter One Summary

- The Four types of Love: Friendship, Passion, Unconditional, Admiration, and the bonus: Wabi-Sabi
- What makes people fall in love: Vulnerability, Trust
- Women look for: Security, Safety, Stability, Empathy, Acceptance.
- Men look for: One who listens, is compassionate, connects physically, validation, respect
- The 7 Elements of Love: Vulnerability, Trust, Connecting, Chemistry of Love, Closeness, Playfulness, Sexuality
- The 10 Emotional Needs: Affection, Sexual Fulfillment, Conversation, Recreational Needs, Honesty, Physical attractiveness, Financial support, Domestic Support, Family Commitment, Admiration.

Chapter Two:

Dysfunctional Basics: Name Yours

"Whenever two people meet there are really six people present. There is each person as they see themselves, each person as the other person sees them, and each person as they really are."

-William James

We know what makes a relationship great, fun and all unicorns and rainbows, so how and why do they fail? What breaks a relationship that was born in bliss and transforms it into a confusing mess, falling down into a pit of insensitivity?

There is usually nothing sudden about it. We don't gain weight overnight and relationship decay occurs just as insidiously and slowly. In this chapter we are going to discuss the signs of dysfunction, connection styles and a host of communication nuances that may be sabotaging your connection and growth. If we were to peel away all the issues, past mistakes and missteps most couples face during the dissolution of their relationshiop, we can sum up ineffective communication as a common denominator.

Communication challenges come is wide variety of flavors. Not communicating enough, emotional attachment to words, outcomes or feelings, or a myriad of issues regarding the interaction itself are all stem from poor communication. When a couple fails to stay emotionally connected to the relationship through the conflict of communication, they are off target before they even attempt a resolution. It is our connection with these other factors (emotion, volume, meaning, outcomes), that cause most communication to derail.

Communication is not simply talking, but knowing how to talk, how to start a conversation, and how to continue to communicate through conflict and love alike. The manner of a couple's communication, or lack thereof, can predict who has some troubling times ahead for them.

PROBLEM VS. PATTERN

It is important to distinguish between a problem and a pattern. Problems are an integral part of any relationship. How we cope with problems becomes a pattern for resolution. It takes concerted effort, at first, to disconnect your feelings during a high level discussion. Getting to an enlightened state where you can sincerely agree to disagree without disdain and anger is our goal. When an "enlightened" couple become keenly aware of their issue and detach their feelings from it, what's left is a clinical and clear path to resolution.

Fighting becomes a discussion and disagreements become an honest and authentic avenue for growth.

When you can discuss a previously touchy subject objectively, you'll begin to revere the crack in your partner's vase and enjoy a vibrant and passionate relationship that does not suffer from boredom, anger or annoyance. When you achieve this level of engagement, you'll have a level of awareness, commitment, loyalty and love that comes only when both parties step back and assess, understand, accept and grow. Just as your bliss may have disintegrated to disdain over time, rebuilding your relationship requires won't happen overnight.

It also rarely occurs without the right tools and training.

When problems keeps recurring, if arguments or conflicts keep rearing their ugly head, placing you into a dysfunctional dance on a regular basis, then the challenge itself may not be the problem. In nearly all cases of relationship meltdown, the *manner and style* in which problems are resolved is often the real culprit, not the perceived issue.

Before we can create the bliss and strength of a solid relationship, however, we must first learn to recognize when our problems have become patterns leading us into that dysfunctional dance. Before you and your partner can sweep away your past challenges and step into the passion and love you both desire, be brutally honest with what isn't working now and what didn't work in the past. We don't need to spend an inordinate amount of time here, but in order to NOT repeat the mistakes of the past, one needs to acknowledge what wasn't working before.

In order to install a new operating system in your relationship, you must first uninstall the old programs that are obsolete. To do that, you need to know which ones they are.

Signs Of Dysfunction

There are several common communication signals that will fire when trouble may be brewing. Every couple has their arguments and conflicts, but the manner in how they are dealt with comes first. If we don't have a deep sense of who we are and how we communicate, we are doomed to repeat this poor coping strategy regardless of the topic of "discussion." Below, we'll discuss several scenarios that may feel awkwardly familiar. You may relate to one or more of these. When most people read them, the first person that comes to mind is their partner. *"Hey, honey... that sounds just like YOU!"*

While it is impossible *not* to think about your partner's dysfunction, we encourage you to read this chapter twice. The first time read it for a general understanding of the problem. During your second read, take your time and do an honest evaluation on how one or more of these styles relates to your current communication challenge. If you have trouble, ask your partner! When you are ready to accept a non-judgmental evaluation of your areas for improvement, the corrupt "program" can be isolated and you'll be ready to install V2.0.

There are dozens of dysfunctional "dances" human beings fall into. Below arre six common ones that most people at one time or another, have some experience with:

➤ The Harsh Startup
➤ The Four Horsemen
➤ Flooding
➤ Body Language
➤ Failed Repair Attempts
➤ Altered Memories

The Harsh Startup

Does one partner begin a conversation with a harsh tone? Something negative or accusatory? This sort of beginning dooms the conversation from the start. Studies have shown that the majority of our communication is non-verbal. The cues we get through body language and "tone" have more to do with understanding a person's point of view as opposed to the actual words being used.

Before reflecting on your partner's harsh tone, consider your own... How would you like it if the other person screamed out their complaint to you? Humans naturally go on the defensive when attacked, both physically and verbally. What if that same person approached you with a softer tone and a more positive attitude? How would that affect your communication?

Compare, *"You forgot to take out the Trash. Again!"* to a far more gentler, *"Oh, the trash isn't emptied yet and I've got the kids to deal with. Do you mind? Thanks."* One of these starts a fight, while the other one will probably end with, *"Sure, hon. But I've got to be off to work after that."*

The Four Horsemen[1]

Best selling author, John Gottman refers to as the Four Horsemen of an apocalyptic relationship. Starting up conversations on a negative note can lead the relationship through a series of four types of negative interactions he calls, the Four Horsemen:

- Criticism
- Contempt

---

[1]Dr. John Gottman, The Marriage Clinic

- Defensiveness
- Stonewalling

Criticism is different from complaining. We all have at least a little complaint about someone, but a criticism differs in how these complaints are expressed. A complaint focuses on one specific behavior- you didn't take out the trash, you left the seat up on the toilet again, for example. A criticism attacks the character of the person. You are so selfish, you're just a lazy bum, you are inconsiderate, and so on. Criticism happens from time to time, but having too much of it can lead to the second horseman; contempt.

Contempt communicates disgust at the person it is intended for, not only in words but body language. Eye rolling or smirks, coupled with sarcasm, name-calling, and mockery are all body language signals of contempt. When contempt is in one's heart, it is impossible to resolve the conflict because the one with contempt is not open to the possibility of resolution. The contempt acts as a barrier to healing.

Contempt causes the other partner to become *defensive*. This puts the blame back on the criticizer but never solves the problem at hand and creates more escalation of discourse. Eventually one partner tunes the other out, which leads to our fourth horseman; *Stonewalling*. More common in men than in women, it is a way of avoiding the flood of negativity as a conflict escalates. The stonewaller ignores his partner, showing no signs of responding, which of course makes his partner all the angrier.

Stonewalling itself is crticized and the vicious cycle is complete. The man may go off by himself in an effort to not react or show his anger, but the wife perceives this as being ignored and rejecting her, which begins the cycle. The wife complains, the husband withdraws, and so the wife complains the more.

To avoid the Four Horsemen in the first place, you need a strong base of love and respect to overcome any negativity and learn how to properly deal with any conflict. There are clear strategies for avoiding and/or repairing this disempowering cycle or pattern. Our WE^3 immersion retreats have a 92%+ rate of success for permanently eliminating this downward spiral of dysfunction for couples. It doesn't matter if you are having your first fight or are filing divorce papers that week, when couples take the steps to understand and positively cope with their "virus-laden" patterns, a new program is ready to be installed.

In addition to the "Four Horsemen" there are other negative coping patterns and signals that you may recognize in yourself or your partner.

Flooding

Another negative pattern of coping is when one partner becomes flooded by so much negativity by the other they become shell-shocked. This causes them to emotionally disengage or stonewall to protect themselves.

Flooding is similar to being at school as a kid, when the bullies just keep at you day in and day out. Enough people yelling and teasing you to the point where you want to crawl under a rock for self-preservation. As adults it can still happen, only the bully isn't a kid on the playground, but your partner. Being under constant attack, what would you *expect* the other person to do? There's only so much negativity that one can take before they just say "Enough!" and go off somewhere to disconnect from the world.

If you see signs that you or your partner is being flooded, ease up for a while. Ease up a *lot*. You don't have to resolve all conflicts immediately. Sometimes, the proper thing to do is nothing. When a flood is occurring, the best strategy may be to let the rain subside before attempting to dry out the basement.

Body Language

There are physiological changes in the body that accompany flooding and other negative reactions, including increased blood pressure, heart rate and adrenaline that makes it impossible to maintain any discussion in a civil manner. When a person is visibly upset, it becomes harder to pay attention to what the other is saying or figure a way to intellectually resolve the situation. The other person often reacts more out of reflex then logic. This reactive response is readily apparent in their body language.

Ever seen someone's face flush red with anger? Or too angry to properly form words? It's a physiological fact that emotions affect your body and metabolism. You might twitch when you feel nervous or feel that fluttering in your stomach. Depression leaves you feeling like lead and having a complete lack in energy.

Likewise when you're angry. Anger triggers the instinctive fight or flight mode your body is hard wired for. The pulse quickens, adrenaline floods the body, preparing you for a fight, and the thinking part of your brain is shut out of the conversation. The same holds true when a high-security computer system detects a virus; all connections are shut down as the anti-virus software starts hunting it down. You are in a state of war, ready to take on all attackers, even if it happens to be your spouse, and the signs of such readiness will display clearly in your body language for the alert person to see.

Failed Repair Attempts

When one partner tries to make amends through an apology, laughter or anything to ease the tension, but the other consistently refuses due to being flooded, the attempted repair becomes futile. The flooded partner has completely disengaged from the discussion. In fact, such repair attempts may be seen as just another part of the argument. That laugh may be seen as the partner being laughed *at,* or the joke possibly at their expense. Everything will be seen through storm-tinted glasses and the repair attempt simply makes things worse.

Altered Memories

The final sign is when a couple recalls their past with a negative view, see "signs" that should have warned them of the bad times to come, or even changed the way they remember things to correspond to their current negative view on the relationship. The excess negativity has led to a distorted view of their past. The "good times" are reduced or even forgotten showing no sign of success and a future with no roadmap to a better tomorrow.

The antidote for these signs of dysfunction is simple but will require practice. It doesn't matter if you've been having challenges for 3 weeks or 3 years, restoring love and creating a solid relationship will always require change, adaptability and the resolve to love and respect each other.

To overcome any amount of negativity, listen to and validate the other person. Have sincere empathy for them. It is impossible to learn a new dance without the occasional "stepping on the other's toes", so just apologize and continue dancing. No need to stop the tango because of a bruised piggy. Just laugh it off and try a new step. There are no judges watching your dance moves.

Enjoy the music.

"The greatest asset to the human experience is the ability to navigate one's emotions. By practicing the skill of detachment, one can successfully step back from the potentially destructive and tune into the purely positive."

– Gary Hopkins

ATTACHMENT STYLES[2]

To understand what can break up a relationship it's important to understand how it came into being. What motivated someone to go from being single (an "I") to becoming a couple (a "We")? The style in which a couple imprinted upon one another, the style of attachment that formed between them has as more to do with their bond than physical attraction or common interests. To better understand the "We" (you as a couple) it is imperative to clearly understand the "I" (you as an individual) as well.

How do you connect?

When you bond with a person, each bond or attachment is manifested in our own unique manner. There are many attachment styles to understand before we can grow towards the most stable style.

---

[2] John Bowlby, Secure Base

The style of attachment one forms depends a great deal on their upbringing. Our early childhood experiences color the way we interpret the world; if it's dangerous or safe, if they are lovable or unlovable. We are hardwired to seek love and comfort, to seek secure attachments, but how we view the world and ourselves alters the view.

We don't "attach" to ourselves, but to another person. Your attachment style may or may not be the same as your partner. Take a look at the styles below and before you jump to the "We" of your relationship, sit back and reflect on how *you* attach. Keep in mind you may have more than one style, but for your current relationship, there will be a dominant style that is giving you false comfort, angst, discourse, or even bliss.

➢ The Anxious Connector
➢ The Avoidance Connector
➢ The Pleaser Connector
➢ The Controller and Victim Connection
➢ The Fearful Connector
➢ The Vacillator Connector
➢ The Secure Connector

The Anxious Connector

The anxious connector feels unlovable and insecure and they quickly pursue connections with others, with a worry that it might all go away. They are quick to take the blame, feeling inadequate, leading to a demanding and dependent style. They are desperate for attachment, yet doomed to feel it can never be achieved. When a person yearns out of fear instead of love, their pursuit can push their partner away. That which they fear often comes to fruition because when they chase too an extreme, the other party may feel confined.

The Avoidant Connector

This personality limits their dependency on others. They are uncomfortable with closeness and prefer to be self-sufficient. They feel worthy of love, connect very carefully and avoid certain emotions that may trigger attachments. Usually this is someone who has had a history of trauma or grew up in a family where they didn't have a secure environment, trust, or where there was abuse. They would like to have love but don't "need" it. They prefer a positive image of their self, and distance themselves from others to maintain it. They protect themselves from rejection. This loner mentality is an archetype for many male roles in action movies (Think "Dirty Harry" or "Iron Man") where a person's independence takes detachment to an extreme. Instead of being detached with the capability of love, the person detaches to the exclusion of vulnerability, trust and, of course, love.

The Pleaser Connector

If you were the "good kid" growing up, you are the Pleaser. Pleasers have a passion to please others and avoid rejection. As an adult you do the same but at the expense of your own needs. Pleasers often have difficulty tolerating space and separation. Emotional and physical distance from your spouse will result in feelings of insecurity, anxiety, and jealousy. When others are upset, you are the first to try and soothe the situation, and express anger indirectly. After a while, the Pleaser may become resentful at giving more than they get, even when your spouse tells you that you keep giving things he/she doesn't want. You need to just say "No" and learn to tolerate the conflict that may arise from being honest. Express your own feelings and needs for change. Being a pleaser has its limits and before things boil over, be sure to take a breath and take care of yourself.

The Controller And Victim Connectors

If your parents were controlling, that created extra stress when you were a child. As a Victim, you learned to defend yourself through aggression and control. Even anger was preferable to shame, humiliation, and grief. As an adult, the only mechanisms you understand is to control others by using threats, intimidation, or even violence. Any sign of insecurity is banished by a quick wave of anger. However, this anger is merely a mask for past grief.

If you survived the chaos of your childhood by being compliant and passive, or even invisible, as an adult you may still feel unable to assert yourself. Victims often marry someone controlling and domineering. Low self-esteem reinforces your belief that all problems are your fault, so you try even harder to suppress your anger in front of your spouse. To get out of your emotional rut, find a safe place to gain confidence and support.

The Fearful Connector

This type connects very cautiously, fearful of closeness, and very concerned about being abandoned. They feel others are untrustworthy, hurtful, and unable to love them, and that emotions are scary and overwhelming. They view others as uncaring and themselves as unlovable, and will avoid intimacy because they expect rejection. When a person acts and reacts from a place of fear, the other party may not recognize why they are attracted or repulsed by the person. (If they are attracted, they often come from a "rescuer" mentality. If they are repulsed, they revere independence and a stalwart personality)

The Vacillator

Vacillator's are keenly aware of their desire for connection and prefer passion and close bonding. These initial intense connections, however, causes one to idealize others which sets you up for disappointment and feeling rejected and unwanted. The vacillating between the need for attention and feeling too angry to receive it begins; sending mixed signals to your mate who feels they are walking on eggshells. As a vacillator, you may recognize multiple love styles for yourself! (Another reason you vacillate) Focus on becoming aware of your emotions and being objective. The more you understand and detach a bit from the feelings, the clearer you will become on your needs.

The Secure Connector

This is the safe haven of attachments. Couples who can display emotions without fear have a secure attachment style. They are comfortable with being close, and don't fear abandoned when they area not. A secure individual has a positive view of themselves, their spouse, and others. A Secure Connector can establish close relationships and use others as support when needed. There is a sense of trust, safety, and love. When both people are secure, their connection may appear aloof. However, the security each feels in their "I" space is strong enough that the "We" has limited fear and anxiety of loss.

A secure connector is comfortable with balance. They are equally content with giving and receiving in a marriage. They recognize the strengths and weaknesses in themselves and others without idealizing or devaluating. Secure Connectors had good examples of resolving conflict as a child and therefore, feel natural doing so in their marriage. The Secure Connecgtor is not afraid to apologize when wrong. They know They're not perfect and are comfortable with new situations, willing and ready to improve themselves in any of these areas in which they may be lacking.

Sounds almost perfect…or impossible.

In reality, becoming a Secure Connector is a level anyone can achieve. Even a person with severe childhood or adult trauma can transcend their baggage and establish connections with themselves and others securely. Becoming a secure connector requires an internal awareness of why you say, think and do what you do. It will require some "rebooting" of your internal operating system, but once installed and executed (practice with your spouse), you'll be relaxed, secure and share a deep understanding of each other.

Talk with your partner. Ask them which dance steps you have been following and begin to consider a step back to rethink a few of your dance moves.

6 Core Human Needs

We all have our needs, and there are six core human needs that we all have to varying degrees. It is when these needs are not being met or not being communicated properly or listened to that causes conflicts to arise. In any relationship, these needs should be kept in mind by both parties.

- Love/connection/belonging
- Significance/separateness
- Certainty/truth/comfort/safety
- Uncertainty/variety/mystery/adventure/ambiguity
- Growth- Relational, Spiritual, Emotional, Cognitive, & Physical
- Contribution- To others and from others

Which of these stand out for you?

We all have these needs, but we also manifest them in different areas of our lives. The manner in which we express them depends upon many factors. How does your background and sex play into the priority of these needs for you? Generally speaking, women need more connection/belonging, while men are in need of greater significance/independence. Deprive one partner in a relationship of one of their core needs and the seeds of dysfunction will have been planted, the rhythm of the dance disrupted. The computer program of your love will slow or freeze up.

If a man needs independence and a woman needs belonging, how can we possibly get along?

The answer is the question, "To what degree do you require each of these needs?" And, in what areas do you need to express them? As mentioned, we ALL have ALL of these needs. Each individual person has a varying degree of priority and association to these needs. Mr. "Independent" still has a need for certainty in his life. It is only that his need for certainty may manifest in a different area than his partner or spouse. Similarly, Ms.

"Belonging" also has a need for uncertainty in her life! She may crave the security of a relationship, but also needs the uncertainty or surprise of flowers on her table or a weekend away to spice up her romance.

In the above example, a woman's desire for uncertainty can be created inside the certainty of her solid relationship. Her man's need for uncertainty (adventure) may be 100% isolated from his relationship. He may be comfortable expressing his need for adventure within the parameters of work or his hobby instead of the bedroom. The Secure Connected couple understands these needs and applies them in a healthy manner so as not to damage the relationship.

When our 6 core needs are examined and isolated from our actions and habits, it is easy to see what appears to be the problem is not the *real* problem at all. We all have conflict, but what we often don't see very clearly is the core of the conflict is the disassociation of unmet needs. When this isn't clear, confusion is the result.

Confusion of core needs and their improper allocation can spiral down into fear. Not fear in the sense of personal safety, but emotional fear that becomes our "buttons" that our partner can inadvertently push to aggravate us.

These fears are related to our core human needs, the fear that one of them could be taken away from us. For example, most women have a core fear related to disconnection, of not being heard or valued and somehow losing the love of another. For men, it is helplessness, or feeling controlled. They fear failing and getting used by others, of becoming "the little guy".

When someone pushes your fear button, you react with unhealthy words or actions that try to get the other person to change and give you what you want. Your reaction, in turn, triggers the core fear of the other person, who then reacts much as you did, and thus the dance of fear begins. It is an angry and disconnected dance that threatens to crash the relationship server completely.

Everyone has their own needs, but there is a collection of needs that are common to *all* people, the core needs that spell out the definition of humanity. Know these needs, remember them, then see what might be missing from both sides of the relationship. Let's list them first in brief then talk about them and how their absence can be the distance stretching between a couple.

These are the key needs to be happy, the needs we must contribute to fulfilling in our partner, one in the other. For instance, the couple needs to know that they are going to be safe and comfortable in the future; you can't be happy if you are uncertain about things. To achieve this you must avoid risks and carefully plan for the future, be careful of each other, and take care of yourselves. But if you only seek after this certainty, you lose sight of the fact that the future is uncertain. Too much seeking for the absolutely certain may lead you to avoid other desires.

If you must be absolutely certain about someone before taking that first step, then you'll never meet someone at all. You limit your experiences and have trouble falling in love, or have trouble connecting more closely to your partner for fear the effort will cause you more pain. This need for certainty can make some people too controlling, and the cost of it is a loss of spontaneity and life in the relationship. This can lead the spouse to withdraw their admirations and feel that she loves you but does not respect you.

How devastating is it to be loved yet not admired? Or the other way around, to be admired by your partner yet not loved? With only the first we might find we have simply married a "bed buddy" or someone that will love and look after us like a mother and not a wife, while the latter leads to, "Well, we can still be friends." You need both in a relationship; that love and that significance. When you have that, then she feels the love and connection, the belonging, safety, and comfort, and is now motivated to return to him some kind of reward. He in turn then feels admired and motivated to love and connect the more. It becomes an energizing cycle of positive energy that pulls them closer quicker and quicker.

But leave out either the love or admiration and the cycle starts in reverse, pushing you farther and farther away. He is not motivated to admire because she is too controlling, so in the end there is loss of the other core needs.

- ❖ Without Love or Connection, there is no relationship.
- ❖ Without Significance, one partner becomes lost within the shadow of the other and the relationship is no longer a partnership.
- ❖ Without Truth and Certainty there is fear.
- ❖ Without Variety, the relationship becomes dull and grey.
- ❖ Without Growth, there is its opposite.
- ❖ And without Contribution there is a sense of lack of purpose and any reason for being in the relationship in the first place.

Sometimes we didn't get all of our core needs growing up, so we seek them more strongly as adults, sometimes to the detriment of the one we love by stepping on a few of *her* needs. We let the past intrude into our present, which makes it hard to focus on anything in the here and now. We try to solve this in therapy by giving couples exercises that can teach them how to mediate problems, connect more, and meet one another's core needs.

Let's break it down.

The first step begins when you hurt, when you're emotionally wounded. You feel emotions that range from bewilderment, sadness, and disconnection, to anger, frustration, and embarrassment. Naturally you want to feel better, and often that is the expectation that the other person will change to satisfy you, that they will follow your lead in this dance. That is your solution, to change them. (He may say, "Honey, you seem sad. Cheer up! Things could be worse, you know.")

This conflict stirs powerful emotions within you, touching specific fears of connecting, perhaps not feeling attractive enough, of being accepted or simply not being good enough. Your fears reflect in your wants, so when they are touched upon you react. (She may think, *Why doesn't he recognize why I am sad? I can't cheer up…I need to express my sadness and he doesn't allow me to do that! He doesn't understand me at all. Why is he so distant?*)

When someone pushes our fear buttons, we react to seize control. This reaction can take the form of criticism, contempt, defensiveness, or any of the previously given signs of dysfunction. We start pushing their fear buttons and the dance takes another step backward. It begins a forward and back cycle that leaves a couple feeling confused, hurt, and angry, until they have left the dance floor in different directions.

The dance continues not simply because of our own fears,

but how we *react* to them. When someone pushes our fear button, do we really need to push back? Or can we simply show a little love and respect and hope our partner changes his or her dance step? As the saying goes, it takes two to tango. It is important to understand and identify this vicious downward cycle for what it truly is. It is time to install some upgraded software in our relationship system and improve the communication and start dancing more effortlessly.

The exact steps of this dance are written by our attachment and love styles and how it interacts with that of our partner. Do we fear losing him, or fear getting too close? When they try to get closer, does that push our button; activating our fear of closeness? Or, if they seem to draw away does that touch upon another fear button? We may begin the dance by not even being aware we have pushed the other's button, then become confused when they push back.

The phrase dysfunctional dance is incredibly appropriate.

For example, a pursuer trying to get the love of another may unknowingly be going after a withdrawer. The withdrawer, however, feels overwhelmed by the pursuer's emotion, and helpless in pleasing his or her partner. They then withdraw to find peace and calm, which causes the pursuer to feel hurt and rejected, and so she reacts by pursuing the chosen target even more vigorously or risk abandonment and loneliness. Mutual fear buttons have been pushed and the dance of fear begins.

This complex little tango can begin without either party being aware the other took the first step, but the cure is simple enough. Be aware and considerate of your partner's emotional state and needs, show love and respect, and watch your feet on the dance floor. Above all, remember that your dance is just a dance…there is no one judging you and you can always try a different song to get into the swing of things.

Personality Problems

Some problems in a relationship can be traced to personality disorders of one partner or the other. Sometimes something minor such as the inability to trust other people or having a difficult time forgiving. These roadblocks can usually be traced to a trauma the person had earlier in life that is affecting their current relationship. Maybe they hold grudges because of something they experienced long ago, or they have trouble trusting because of some long past abandonment issue. Some of these problems are minor and easily solved, some are more serious and others may need to be looked into professionally.

For example, some men are *passive-aggressive.* To most people this is just a label, so let us drop in a definition. To be considered as a passive-aggressive, you must have four or more of the following:

- Criticize and/or scorn your parents, teachers, and boss without reason.
- Express envy or resentment towards others who are better off than you.
- Exaggerate and complain.
- Exhibit a constantly negative attitude.
- You procrastinate; forget to do things on purpose.
- Fail to do your share of the work or complain that others don't understand or appreciate you.
- Sulk and argue a lot.

Most of us have one or two of these traits, but if you have four of more of these then you may be diagnosed as passive-aggressive. Being with a passive-aggressive means you are really going to start compromising the way you communicate and your needs as an individual.

The passive-aggressive personality trait can be made to change, however, but you have to be careful. Anytime the passive-aggressive lies, gives excuses, or procrastinates, simply tell him how that action affects the relationship, being very specific about how you felt and what you believed. Be careful not to antagonize him or you may just make the situation worse. Work *with* him, show some love and forgiveness, praise them when they keep their promises, and remember that it won't happen overnight but it *will* happen. When he is aggressive, show there will be consequences or he will never learn from his actions. For instance, when he's aggressive tell him the consequence will be you staying at your mother's house for the weekend. With a passive-aggressive you must be firm, clear, and unemotional.

Another personality type is the *non-confrontational* type. The non-confrontational personality is often meek and avoids confrontation at all costs. If only one person is this way, they will often be the one being abused and stepped on by the other, but in the rare example that both are prone to avoiding confrontation, the result can be a miserable relationship.

The meek may inherit the Earth, but when it comes to resolving conflicts, they rarely live true to themselves. Their condition is the result of some experiences earlier in life, something they must be made to go back and face. He must deal with it before he can deal with others, and then reintroduce him to himself. Oftentimes this is a person living so long avoiding confron-

Barbara & Bob

One of our clients is a couple named Barbara and Bob. Bob is an engineer for an aerospace company and Barbara is a stay at home mom. The couple has 3 children and live in Orange County, CA. Barbara was raised by her parents in Glenview, IL by a father who was in the military. Her mother passed away when she was 15 and her dad never remarried.

Bob was raised in Northern California by his parents who were both software engineers. A loving, but quiet couple, Bob learned early on to embrace the silence of peace.

The couple has been married 13 years when they realized that 7 years of issues had been building and neither wanted to talk about them. Barbara's personality had been engrained to be submissive to her husband and Bob had been "trained" to quietly accept life as it happened. Neither was comfortable with discussing the marriage.

Their mutual avoidance nearly ended their marriage.

In fact, Barbara was having a deep emotional affair with a single dad down the street. It started innocently enough. The kids had play dates and they got along like best buddies. Thomas would often watch all their kids while Barbara ran errands and she would make lunch for both families on occasion. Their "friendship" was 100% innocent, plutonic and, so they thought, safe.

However, when Barbara started looking forward to spending time with Thomas as opposed to Bob, she eventually realized she was having an emotional affair. Too embarrassed to talk about her feelings with Bob, she confided in her pastor who referred her to a counselor.

It took her over 4 months to finally talk with Bob about her challenges. Today, these two are still a quiet couple. Their personalities didn't change. However, by becoming aware of their styles, they were able to use their newfound knowledge to build a stronger relationship, as opposed to getting their needs met outside of the marriage.

tation that they do not even know themselves, but are just sleep-walking through life.

The *narcissist* can be a great danger to any relationship, depending on how extreme his case is. The narcissist thinks more of him or her self than anything else, so naturally that person will refuse to accept that anything is wrong with them since they are perfect. This makes it difficult to treat the dysfunction in the relationship, since you have to get them to recognize that they have faults as well.

There are nine different stages of narcissism, the worst level being number 9. That is the level that is fraught with the most danger for the other party and one you must avoid. Run as far and as fast as you can away from them for they will get up and hog the entire dance floor. The true narcissist has an overwhelming drive to impress others, will move Heaven and Earth to be loved and admired, and have blinders on when it comes to taking a really close look at themselves in the mirror. For the stage 9 narcissist, short of a lobotomy they are not going to change… ever or for anyone. They will belittle and manipulate the other person in their relationship and control the situation to the extent where their spouse is in a constant need to impress the narcissist. The partner either becomes an enabler or is forced to leave. There is no positive way of dealing with a *true* narcissist.

There are hundreds of other personality types that can damage a relationship and these are but a few examples. We list these here to give you a sense of how complicated relationships can become when you avoid the basics and dwell on the other person's issues. Imagine a non-confrontational person with a passive-aggressive, or a passive-aggressive with a narcissist. The more of a negative personality type that one is, the more of a positive type the partner must be in order to deal with him and find a way to mend the problems of both that person and their relationship.

If you don't start with becoming a better 'you', creating a better 'we' is impossible.

DEALING WITH DYSFUNCTION

Recognizing the reason behind the problem will show you how to deal with it effectively. In Chapter Six we will examine the different coping strategies that people employ to get through a less-than-perfect relationship, but first you have to know how to spot what strategy (for better or worse) you are using to cope. Like the hen-pecked husband who submits just enough to mollify the wife, his strategy "works" by bending to instead of dealing directly with her unmet needs. Conversely, the strategy of the henpecked husband who resorts to drinking excessively also "works" but has a completely different residual effect. Dealing with dysfunction becomes another step in the dance, but sometimes our steps get caught in a circle with no way out and we find ourselves stuck in the same unproductive routine.

Like a computer, our brains are hardwired to form attachments and be social, but sometimes too much junk gets downloaded that slows things down. When we download a coping strategy to mollify our spouse, the relationship doesn't 'crash' but it certainly does not run optimally. Worse, of course, is the husband who drinks to avoid the real issue; the relationship virus will eventually crash the system. A coping strategy that uses a tool like alcohol has nowhere to go but down. Much like a computer system that freezes up with a virus, the only cure is a reboot. Some couples may be able to reboot their relationship with a simple 'software' upgrade located within the words of this book. Most, however, would benefit tremendously and save tens of thousands of dollars by participating in one of our exclusive WE³ immersion retreats. For information and to see if you qualify, visit our free membership at, www.RelationshipSociety.com.

In either case, the mission is to recognize the pattern behind the trouble, like isolating the virus, then remove it and reboot the relationship. When one person doesn't listen to another, it's like the system requester popping up telling you there is a problem only you're on the other screen ignoring it. All you know is that the program refuses to install and you continue to push buttons, getting angrier, and all the while that one icon is blinking at you waiting for a response. Nothing will happen until you face that problem that's stopping everything.

"Awareness is important in that it creates the capacity to choose responses that are different than the ones habitually acted upon, laying the foundation for something new to emerge."

–Joe Whitcomb

We are all responsible for the operating system to our lives and sometimes we just need a bit of clearing out of some excess code, or to continue with our dance analogy, sometimes we discover our shoelaces have gotten tied together and we need to pause to untie them. Not all counselors are qualified to do a complete reboot, mind you. Many strategies we have seen stay within the confines of traditional therapy. Daddy issues, affairs, or other trauma are rarely dealt with properly with a few hours of thought.

While traditional therapy can certainly bring awareness, it has a deplorable record for creating empowering and permanent change for individuals and couples. In fact, the success rate of traditional couples therapy is dismally low. According to Consumer Reports, the only form of therapy that received low ratings in a famous national survey of therapy clients, published in 1996, was couples therapy!

The reason our WE^3 system has such a high success rate is because we immerse the couple in an experiential transformation of entertainment, empowerment and engagement. You can't escape life without challenges and no couple completes our WE^3 program without a complete reboot, new software and an energized, fresh outlook on their relationship. It is only through a complete immersion such as this, that awareness can transform into permanent change.

We use the word transform and not "change", because you cannot change another person. You can change yourself, but not anyone else. Change is about doing, about getting more information and making something happen, while transformation is about being aware, present, and connected; not just to yourself and to the other person. Our proprietary system allows a person to safely work on themselves as individuals and how to properly relate to their partner. This allows a couple to have a "We" instead of a two "I's". In order to create permanent transformation for the couple, we need to change the individual, first. This occurs by taking ownership of their individual strengths and weaknesses and being willing to understand and transform their own patterns so they can better connect up with their partner.

And that leads us to the crux of our process, for you cannot change a relationship without first transforming the individual.

Discovering what needs to be changed is like finding the errors in a computer program, then fixing them before you can reboot the computer and see it run smoothly again; you have transformed the program. For the remainder of this book, our goal will be to help you find the errors in your programming then help you transform yourself so that you can reboot your relationship.

Look upon us as the dance instructor, come into the room to teach you the correct steps so you can go back to your partner and show her you can really cut a rug.

Chapter Two Summary

- Signs of Dysfunction: The Harsh Startup, The Four Horsemen, Flooding, Body Language, Failed Repair Attempts, Convenient Memories
- The Four Horsemen: Criticism, Contempt, Defensiveness, Stonewalling
- Attachment Styles: Secure Connector, Anxious Connector, the Avoidant, Vacillator, Contorller & Victim, Fearful Connector, Secure Connetor.
- Six core Human Needs:
- Love/connection/belonging
- Significance/separateness
- Certainty/truth/comfort/safety
- Uncertainty/variety/mystery/adventure/ambiguity
- Growth- Relational, Spiritual, Emotional, Cognitive, and Physical
- Contribution- To others and from others
- Personality problems in a relationship: Passive-Aggressive, non-confrontational, narcissist
- You cannot change a relationship without transforming the individual.

Chapter Three:

HOW DID WE GO FROM LOVE TO LACK?

"When did 'I love you,' degenerate into
Meet my needs!'?"

We started out head over heels in love, ogling one another with doe-eyed visions of rapture, just the two of us against the World.

Bliss…

Why then do so many people find themselves not wanting to be in the same room with their partner after a few years? How did this happen?

How did we go from Love to Lack?

We are hard-wired to be social beings, to seek our matching halves. However, we are also hard-wired to be a bit selfish, to protect our own interests. The latter stems from our basic survival instincts and can sometimes bring us in conflict with the social-seeking side. This creates a space between you and me, between the "I" and the "We". Love, then, is about the journey through that space, to go from the I to the We, and oftentimes that journey is a rather bumpy road.

We will help you safely transverse the minefield and come out on the other end with a new power, peace, and understanding that can not only return you to the bliss you experienced as a new couple, but strengthen your love to unforeseen levels of joy.

This path, of course, comes with some basic lessons and advanced training. You can't simply read about a few personality quirks, talk about them with your partner and reach harmony overnight. Just as you can't instantly become a tango professional by reading about it, creating secure attachments, establishing deep connections as you both go through the inevitable changes of life, require specific toolsets and practice.

As your awareness increases, you should also increase practicing your new relationship dance so you can become the vibrant, loving couple you both desire.

To seek the "We", the needs of the "I" must not go unfulfilled. As discussed earlier, the 6 core needs of all human being vary from one degree to another. We express them in different ways. One of the seeds of our personal expression of those needs comes from our upbringing. Specifically, our family of origin.

FAMILY OF ORIGIN ISSUES

It is not uncommon for the sins of the father to suffer upon his offspring. The family you come from, the environment in which you were raised, can have a profound affect upon your adult life. Here are a few examples of the types of issues that could stem from your Family of Origin:

- ❖ If your father was a drunk, then that will affect how you view others, perhaps by always being on the alert of anyone ready to abuse you.

- ❖ If you were raised in a tough neighborhood, then you may keep expecting anyone trying to get close to you has ulterior motives.

- ❖ If you were physically or sexually abused as a child, then as an adult you may resort to alcoholism, which in turn passes another problem down to *your* kids.

- ❖ If your parents had a high quality marriage then this will transmit into your own relationships as well.

There are more, but you should get the idea. We are all a product of our environment.

Family of Origin issues affect not only how we live our own private lives, but by extension, how we engage with others. How you make sense of your past experiences and adjust to them will influence the quality of your current and future relationships.

Family of Origin issues affect our current emotional needs and attachment styles. If your father was an angry abuser, your

"Awareness is important in that it creates the capacity to choose responses that are different than the ones habitually acted upon, laying the foundation for something new to emerge."

-Edwin Friedman
Generation to Generation

mother fearful and controlling, then your problems will most likely revolve around anxiety and fear; you will seek someone who can give you a feeling of comfort and security. To advance beyond your Family of Origin issues, you first need to become aware of them. Be honest with yourself; take a look at your past and what your upbringing left within you that you may need to work on.

Being unaware of the issues that lie beneath the way you act and respond is like a computer running its program on full automatic; you have no control and are not acting as a fully thinking being. However, by becoming aware of your core issues, of what lies beneath the undercurrent, you can break free of your trap, program yourself, and rise to the ranks of a fully thinking being. You will be in charge of your present instead of being ruled by your past.

Understanding your Family Of Origin issues is a basic fundamental to understanding yourself and is the key to fixing today's relationship challenges.

IMPRINTS FROM OUR PAST[3]

We often create a story that we keep telling ourselves, one based on something from our past. Quite often, an event justifies how we behave and why we keep past issues alive in our relationships. These issues show up as problems in our Intimacy Triangle. These are imprints from our past. Is our story serving us or can we change the story in order to have the future that we want?

In the example in the last section, Barbara justified her need for another relationship by telling herself that Bob was uncom-

---

[3] Harvel Hendrix, Getting the Love You Want

municative and not fulfilling her emotional needs. Every time she told that story to herself she was validating the affair, but the affair only drove her farther apart from her husband. When told she had to end the affair, she was afraid that she would not have anyone to be close to afterwards. She could not see that in order to reconnect with her husband, she had to disconnect from the affair. She needed a new imprint to replace the one that was keeping her in the affair and away from her husband.

Such an imprint keeps us in an ineffective loop, going nowhere on the dance floor of life, endlesslly going through the motions that lead you nowhere new.

Stop selling yourself the same old story.

An imprint can happen from something in our childhood, a past traumatic experience, or a chronic ongoing influence from our environment. Imprints can affect us subconsciously and change our view of ourselves and the world. Whatever the perception is, whether we understand it or not, the message gets internalized, digested and becomes a part of our being. What comes next is a sense of not belonging, not being a part of something. The final stage of of not belonging is the feeling of being alone.

1) We are affected subconsciously

2) We feel broken

3) The message gets internalized

4) We feel that we don't belong

5) We feel alone

At that point the genesis of our imprint is complete. We may keep testing different situations to see if the pattern changes our story. But without a new set of tools to fix the cycle, nothing changes. History repeats itself. Our vicious cycle affects how we interact with other people and how we let other people interact with us. Regardless of how absurd or illogical the situation is, what we believe becomes our truth.

It becomes a self-fulfilling prophecy.

Let's explore an example of a person with early disconnection and rejection. This individual has a need for security, safety, empathy, and the desire to be accepted. He could come from a background of rejection, abusiveness, or where affection was withheld. These beliefs are internalized as feelings of abandonment, mistrust, emotional deprivation, shame, and social isolation. The individual feels defective or alienated in any relationship. This person's method of dealing with these feelings becomes internalized as an emotional imprint. The person seeks security, safety, and empathy, but no matter how much security and safety is offered, he fully expects to be rejected sooner or later and so prepares himself for "the inevitable" which he then proceeds to cause to come about.

He becomes the cause of his own rejection.

Invalidation is a big one for most people. Everyone has been invalidated in some way, so there is an expectation that one's desire for a normal degree of emotional support will not be sufficiently met by anyone and they will thus feel deprived. There are three major forms of deprivation:

1) Deprivation of nurturance

2) Deprivation of empathy or validation

3) Deprivation of protection

Lacking one of them becomes an internal need to acquire it, to be admired or loved by another. We begin giving to another person to get what we lack in return, but since our lack stems from some unfinished business, that other person can never fulfill our need and so he then becomes the problem. We continue to feel incomplete.

For example, if in our past we had been abused, lied to, humiliated, or hurt in some way, then we have an expectation that the other person is going to do just that to us now; if he happens to do so (even unintentionally) we perceive the harm is intentional and thus our fears are justified. We then have our excuse to break up the relationship because we "saw it coming."

From Savannah:

I was working with a couple where the gal had come into her relationship with a lot of abuse from her mother and father. The father was physically and emotionally abusive, very demanding, and an alcoholic, so there was a lot of instability in her upbringing. Thus she would color the actions of the man that she was with in light of her past, which caused him to become more defensive and shut down and withdraw.

If he was running late, he had problems remembering to call and let her know, and so she would text him again and again, then scold him later, which would cause him to withdraw from their conversations and communicate even less. He wasn't doing anything more than reacting to her constant texting, which she did in fear that he was actually cheating on her the way her father would his mother. He was madly in love with her, there was no way he was going to look at anyone else, but she kept testing to see if he was there for her until it became too controlling and smothering. She had an expectation that he was going to hurt and abuse her and so saw everything he did as evidence to that fact.

If he said, "No, I'm just running late at work," she would think that a lie and evidence that he was indeed cheating on her. She always felt she was getting walked on or abandoned, and in a way was allowing that to happen to her in fulfillment of her own imprint. The more he would try to connect with her and fix things, the more she would see it in the light of her imprint and discount it as something negative.

When dealing with a case like this, as I listen to the couple talk I am paying more attention to the emotional cues beneath their words than to the words themselves; the undercurrent that drives the words, for it is this current that can be followed back to the past imprint that created the feelings in the first place. When there is a problem with your partner; listen to the emotions *beneath* the words and consider the real reason behind them, of the imprint from their past that is creating the emotion in the first place.

Going back to our dance analogy, there are three views to a dance, just as there are three views to a couple's dialogue. There is the way that she dances, the way that he dances, and the way that they dance together. So too there is her view of the dialogue, his view of the dialogue, and what is really going on between them. Process the content of what you are saying to each other. The words and origins between the lines is where discoveries are made and where reconnection occurs.

A Couple's Anniversary Story:

Roger W. was working for a high-end company as a consultant before deciding to go into his own consulting business. His wife, Lilly was extremely supportive of this, as well as the fact of his going for his MBA. Advancing his education should translate into higher income and more security. It was the middle of summer when they were having a conversation about it, and it also happened to be their anniversary. They were trying to plan their anniversary but kept getting boxed in by money, children, and time. After working over 90 hours per week in school and work, Roger finally decided to take the day off to celebrate, treat her to lunch and a movie.

On the same day, Lilly tells him that she needed to take the car to Pep Boys because the car's repair light had come on and she needed $18 for the diagnostic to see what was wrong. Roger, a bit sleepless from his extreme schedule, quickly calculated his budget at $200 and figured it wouldn't break the bank. He gave her the budget, told her to take care of it, that they'd drop it off on the way to lunch and a movie.

The afternoon movie was a welcome retreat. Afterwards, Lilly calls Pep Boys and discovers another diagnostic was needed, one that was going to cost $80. Roger quickly objected, said the car works fine and they could take care of it later. For the next few minutes, Lilly kept pressing, insisting that it needed to get taken care of right away. Roger was focusing on the anniversary afternoon and already determined the budget limit. He held firm and clearly stated, "No. We'll talk about it later." She didn't back down and so the dance began. He quickly became angry enough to cancel the rest of their date and walked off, angry and upset. Lilly was stunned-but calm.

Roger went on to tell me how he was then walking in the promenade when he looked in a mirror and saw his wife kind of smiling. In our couples work, we had taught him to stop, think, and observe what is really going on underneath his reactions and emotions, and he did. He stopped dead in his tracks, went back to her, and told her why he reacted in the manner he did.

He had his fears. He just had two clients drop out over the summer, didn't have the money coming in, and was afraid he would not have the money to support them. He just wanted them to have a great time, but now with this new bill it had become too large a risk.

Lilly's response was a confession of her own, of her own imprint from the past. It was back in 1999 when she was on the highway with their little baby boy in the back seat of the car. The fix-it light was on then and they'd done nothing about it. They were traveling down the 405 freeway, cars coming from behind them at seventy miles an hour, when the car stalled. She thought she was going to die. Ever since then that repair light coming on means they could die if not fixed. That red light held a life-or-death meaning that Roger was absolutely clueless about...until he asked.

The issue them was never about money or getting the car fixed, but something much more important. Once they both realized the root cause of their opinions, they were able to open an honest dialogue and understand one another.

Without angst.

Without stonewalling.

Without judgment.

It ended with Lilly telling him they could put off the repair, but he insisting that they finally get it done. It was an imprint from the past that had gotten between them, and they handled it by validating each other's emotional needs and fears. Roger had risked being vulnerable by confessing his own fears and imperfections about not having enough money and not feeling good enough, and she returned her own vulnerability and trust by opening up about a deep-seated fear of her own.

Dig deep between the meanings of your words and you and your partner will find core issues that can transform not just your communication, but your love. Find it, fix it, and then see how much closer you can begin to connect with your partner.

To borrow from Shakespeare and tweak things a little, "There are more things between you and your spouse than are dreamt of in your subconscious." If some little thing sets one of you off, realize the real seed lies far deeper. In our WE^3 retreats we teach couples how to connect the dots until we find what issues are really at the heart of the matter. The sooner you find the root of the problem, the sooner you can reconnect.

Imprints from the past exercise:

The Imago

MY IMAGO PROFILE

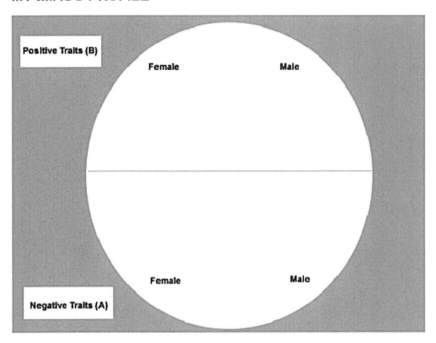

Step One: Thinking as a young child, on the top half of the circle WRITE a list of positive traits of your early caregivers (female on the left side; male on the right side) as you remember them from childhood. CIRCLE the three best positive traits.

Step Two: On the bottom half of the circle, LIST the negative traits of each of your early caregivers (female on the left side; male on the right side) as you remember them from childhood. CIRCLE the three worst negative traits.

Step Three: COMPLETE this sentence: What I wanted and needed most as a child and didn't get was (C) _____

CHILDHOOD FRUSTRATIONS

Frustrations mask an unmet need that often stem from childhood. In the left column below, 1ˢᵗ any recurring frustrations such as "did not get listened to", "no one knew I was being hurt", "had to take care of parents or siblings". On the right, list how you responded to these frustrations. This should be how you felt AND your behavioral response (i.e. what you did).

CHILDHOOD FRUSTRATIONS	E) RESPONSES

POSITIVE CHILDHOOD MEMORIES

WRITE down below three Positive Childhood Memories and the corresponding <u>feeling</u> (see examples below).

SITIVE CHILDHOOD MEMORIES	FEELING
Example: Christmas mornings	Excited
Example: When I hit a home run that won the game.	Proud

My Imago

Using the information from the Finding Your Imago and Childhood Frustrations/Positive Memories of Childhood Memories of Childhood sheet, complete the sentences below. The letters in parenthesis correspond to these sheets and tell you from where to transcribe the information.

I am trying to get a person who is (A) _____

_____

_____

To always be (B) _____

_____

_____

So that I can get (C) _____

_____

_____

And feel (D) _____

_____

_____

I stop myself from getting this sometimes by (E) _____

_____

_____

The Relationship Dance[4]

The conflict between the needs of the "I" versus the "We" become a dance of their own. We fight for connection, for closeness, but we also seek to protect our hearts from being hurt and devalued. When we focus on our own needs without regard to our partners needs simultaneously, we often fall into a rhythm of getting closer and backing away, a cycle through pain and pleasure. Sooner or later one person in this dance cannot stand it anymore and the relationship becomes more detached. We long for closeness and create separation.

Pursuing and withdrawing is a common way that couples relate, but one that often leaves them removed from one another. In their attempt to be seen and understood by their partner, many couples become stuck in this cycle. One partner pursues and the other withdraws, and the *more* one pursues the *more* the other withdraws. Finally, the withdrawer shuts down completely. The dance of dysfunction moves off of the dance floor because they are unable to share what is in their hearts; they are only able to share their anger and frustration. The pursuer feels the loss of the other's attention and so seeks it through a growing haze of anger and frustration, feeling that if he or she does not pursue then the other will go away.

It is quite common for women to be the pursuer. A woman's high level of emotional communication can be perceived as nagging by her man who is often less communicative. Without an answer to a woman's inquiry, she doubles down on her pursuit. Emotions overtake the content and the withdrawer is over-

---

[4] Greg Smalley, DNA of relationships for couples

whelmed by the pursuer's frustration. They both end up feeling devalued and disrespected.

Men are known to use 30 to 50 percent fewer words in a day than women. What is seen by a woman as withdrawing is often a man's frugal use of his vocabulary. The cycle accelerates as her increased frustration does nothing to help him open up and share more. The pursuer pursue's more and the withdrawer withdraws in kind.

When one is busy either pursuing or withdrawing, he or she does not have the energy left to see the partner's perspective and needs. They see one another as inconsiderate and uncaring, that the other does not understand them.

What usually triggers this dance cycle is when something happens that suddenly puts your spouse into a different light.

Dancing On Each Other's Footsteps

Mary is a night owl, while John is an early bird. John interprets Mary's inability to fall asleep at 9 p.m. as uncaring and disrespectful, while Mary views John's request to go to bed with him so early as being unreasonable and insensitive. The difference lies in their internal body clocks, yet each sees it as an inability of the other to be sensitive and caring. This difference can grow to become a threat to their closeness.

Instead of trying to change the other person, each partner must become keenly aware of the other's differences. Relationships aren't merely compromises to one's individuality; like wabi-sabi love, one must learn to embrace the difference (and flaws) of their partner.

Being detached from your interpretation of your partner's quirks and nuances will go a long way to getting your OWN idiosyncrasies identified and embraced by your partners.

In the words of Steven Covey, "In order to be understood, seek first to understand." Love isn't blind. Love is actually the exact opposite... it is intuitive.

You see them as no longer kind or thoughtful, not the loving person that you married, and so you withdraw or pursue. It might not have been what your spouse meant it to seem, but that is the way that you saw it.

When such a difference becomes a threat, the other person is seen as an enemy instead of a companion. The irony is most of the time it was the difference between you two that pulled you together in the first place. It is only the perception of these differences that shifts from positive to negative. Our fear of talking openly where our opinions and feelings are subject to criticism, blame, and defensiveness become roadblocks to the secure connection we actually want.

The way out of this dangerous dance is non-judgemental communication; communication that involves the sharing of your needs, hurts, and feelings in an open, honest and non-emotional fashion. When we speak calmly, with no yelling, it is easier to capture a person's intent, meaning, and feelings. Regardless if you are a withdrawer or a pursuer, expressing your needs and longings will have its difficulties.

Depending on if you are the Withdrawer or the Pursuer, there are a few things that you should keep in mind when communicating.

Withdrawer:

The withdrawer must learn to openly share his feelings and not assume that the other can read their thoughts or emotional states. Your interactions should revolve around your longings and fears, not anger and disappointment. If you don't know what to do, try the following:

- Admit that you do not know what to do.
- Ask your spouse what they need from you.
- If you don't know what you are supposed to do with your spouse's emotions, listen with an empathic attitude.

Even if you can't find a solution to whatever their challenge is, be there for them. Most of the time, a solution isn't the answer. Listening is.

Pursuer:

The pursuer, on the other hand, must learn to express their heart without anger and without being attached to the response of the withdrawer. Try the following:

- Learn to relax
- Breathe
- Allow the withdrawer to take the time and space they need to effectively communicate their feelings without an instant response.
- Count to 10 and ask clarifying questions before offering any answers or solutions.

If you catch yourself trying to "fix" the situation, understand that many withdrawers may simply need to express a frustration or feeling, not necessarily have it "repaired." Sometimes the nod of your head or an affirming "I see" is enough to make the withdrawer comfortable to share more.

When you are first coming out of this withdraw and pursue cycle, it is important to emotionally reconnect as soon as you can. Do not simply sweep the incident under the rug and forget about it, or it may return again later as an unresolved hurt. When trying to reconnect after being hurt, remember these three things:

1) *Acknowledge* what happened: your own role as well as your spouse's role. Admit your part in the conflict.

2) *Share* your hurts and needs, not your anger and frustration.

3) When all is said and done, touch and *Talk*. Soft encouraging tones, a simple soothing touch, can be very powerful.

Of course, if you want to avoid this dance in the first place, there are three things you can do:

1) First, believe in the best intentions of your spouse; don't assume he or she is out to get you.

2) Second, risk doing things differently; open your heart and learn how to relate in ways that draw you together.

3) And finally, decide what it is about your spouse that you love, makes you feel loved and understood by him or her, then *tell* them.

This simple system is a key ingredient to build a closer emotional attachment bond that will weather the pains and pressures of life and marriage, and make of your relationship a safe place to keep your heart.

THE FEAR DANCE

When the relationship dance becomes motivated nearly entirely by your core fears and pushing your spouse's buttons as response, then we have entered into a dangerous cycle of fear. Our relationship dance has become a *fear dance*. Recognizing the symptoms and details of this dance of terror is key to saving your relationship lest you fall into an endless vortex.

Dealing with such a vortex is actually one of the key matters we cover in the WE³ program, but in the meantime, in the next three pages we have attached a worksheet to help you through your cycle of fear and need. Credit for "The DNA of Relationships for Couples" worksheet goes to Greg and Gary Smalley. If you need more help stepping out of your Fear Dance, then the WE³ Program will still be around to assist.

the DNA of RELATIONSHIPS for COUPLES

discovering your core fear

1. Describe a recent conflict, argument, or negative situation with your spouse—something that really "pushed your button."

2. How did you feel in response to this conflict or situation? How did that conflict or argument make you feel? Check all that apply - but "star" the most important feelings:

Unsure	Disappointed	Disgusted	Embarrassed	Other:
Apathetic	Wearied	Resentful	Frightened	
Puzzled	Torn up	Bitter	Anxious	Other:
Upset	Shamed	Fed up	Horrified	
Sullen	Uncomfortable	Frustrated	Disturbed	
Sad	Confused	Miserable	Furious	
Hurt	Worried	Guilty		

3. How did this conflict make you feel about yourself? What did the conflict say about you? What was the "self" message - the message that it sent to you? What were the "buttons" that got pushed? Circle all that apply, but "star" the most important feeling you felt about yourself.

"As a result of the conflict, I felt..."	What That Feeling Sounds Like
Rejected	My spouse doesn't want me; my spouse doesn't need me; I am not necessary in this relationship; my spouse does not desire me; I feel unwanted.
Abandoned	I will be alone; my spouse will ultimately leave me; I will be left alone to care for myself; my spouse won't be committed to me for life.
Disconnected	We will become emotionally detached or separated.
Like a failure	I am not successful at being a husband/wife; I will not perform right or correctly; I will not live up to expectations; I will fall short in my relationship; I am not good enough.
Helpless/powerless	I cannot do anything to change my spouse or my situation; I do not possess the power, resources, capacity, or ability to get what I want; I will be controlled by my spouse.
Defective	Something is wrong with me; I'm the problem.
Inadequate	I am not capable; I am incompetent.
Inferior	Everyone else is better than I am; I am less valuable or important than others.
Invalidated	Who I am, what I think, what I do, or how I feel is not valued.
Unloved	My spouse doesn't love me anymore; my spouse has no affection or desire for me; my relationship lacks warm attachment, admiration, enthusiasm, or devotion; I feel as if we are just roommates—that there are no romantic feelings between us.
Dissatisfied	I will not experience satisfaction within the relationship; in our marriage, I will exist in misery for the rest of my life; I will not be pleased within my marriage; I feel no joy in my relationship.
Cheated	My spouse will take advantage of me; my spouse will withhold something I need; I won't get what I want.
Worthless/devalued	I am useless; I have no value to my spouse.
Don't measure up	I am never able to meet my spouse's expectations of me; I am not good enough as a spouse.
Unaccepted	My spouse does not accept me; my partner is not pleased with me; my spouse does not approve of me.

Judged	I am always being unfairly judged or misjudged; my spouse forms faulty or negative opinions about me; I am always being evaluated; my spouse does not approve of me.
Humiliated	This marriage is extremely destructive to my self-respect or dignity.
Ignored	My spouse will not pay attention to me; I will be unknown in my marriage; I feel neglected.
Unimportant	I am not important to my mate; I am irrelevant, insignificant, or of little priority to my spouse.
Other:	_____

4. What do you do when you feel _____ [insert the most important feeling from question #3]? How do you react when you feel that way? Identify your common coping strategies to deal with your "buttons" being pushed. Check all that apply—but "star" the most important reactions:

Withdrawal	You avoid others or alienate yourself without resolution; you sulk, use the silent treatment.
Escalation	Your emotions spiral out of control; you argue, raise your voice, fly into a rage.
Earn-it mode	You try to do more to earn others' love and care.
Negative beliefs	You believe your spouse is far worse than is really the case; you attribute negative motives to your spouse.
Blaming	You place responsibility on others, not accepting fault; you're convinced the problem is your spouse's fault.
Exaggeration	You make overstatements or enlarge your words beyond bounds or the truth.
Tantrums	You have a fit of bad temper.
Denial	You refuse to admit the truth or reality.
Invalidation	You devalue your spouse; you do not appreciate who your partner is, what he or she feels or thinks or does.
Defensiveness	Instead of listening, you defend yourself by trying to provide an explanation.
Clinginess	You develop a strong emotional attachment or dependence on your spouse.
Passive-aggression	You display negative emotions, resentment, and aggression in unassertive passive ways, such as procrastination and stubbornness.
Caretaking	You become responsible for others by giving physical or emotional care and support to the point you are doing everything for your spouse and your partner does nothing to care for himself or herself.
Acting out	You engage in negative behaviors or addictions like drug or alcohol abuse, extra-marital affairs, excessive shopping or spending, or overeating.
Fix-it mode	You focus almost exclusively on what is needed to solve the problem.
Complain/criticize	You express unhappiness or make accusations; you present a "laundry list" of faults about your mate.
Striking out	You become verbally or physically aggressive, possibly abusive.
Manipulation	You pursue your mate to get them to do what you want; you control your spouse for your own advantage.
Anger or rage	You display strong feelings of displeasure or violent and uncontrolled emotions.
Catastrophize	You use dramatic, exaggerated expressions to depict that the relationship is in danger or that it has failed.
Emotionally shut down	You numb out emotionally; you become devoid of emotion, or you have no regard for other's needs or troubles.
Humor	You use humor as a way of not dealing with the issue at hand.
Sarcasm	You use negative humor, hurtful words, belittling comments, cutting remarks, or demeaning statements.
Minimization	You assert that your spouse is overreacting to an issue; you intentionally underestimate, down play, or soft pedal the issue.
Rationalization	You attempt to make your actions seem reasonable; you try to attribute your behavior to credible motives; you try to provide believable but untrue reasons for your conduct.
Indifference	You are cold and show no concern.
Abdication	You give away responsibilities.
Self-abandonment	You desert yourself; you neglect you; you run yourself down.
Other:	_____

the fear dance

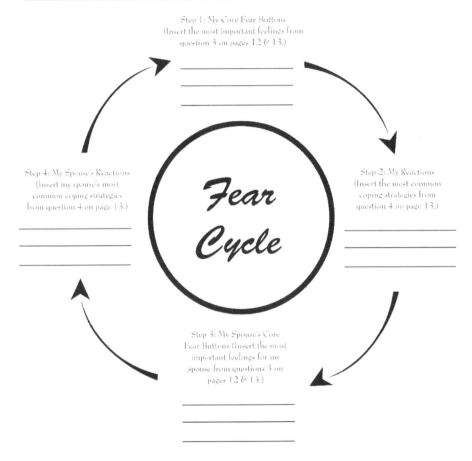

Step 1: My Core Fear Buttons
(Insert the most important feelings from
question 3 on pages 12 & 13.)

Step 2: My Reactions
(Insert the most common
coping strategies from
question 4 on page 13.)

Step 3: My Spouse's Core
Fear Buttons (Insert the most
important feelings for my
spouse from questions 3 on
pages 12 & 13.)

Step 4: My Spouse's Reactions
(Insert my spouse's most
common coping strategies
from question 4 on page 13.)

Fear Cycle

Step 5: Discuss how this dance plays out in your conflicts.

THE 10 EMOTIONAL NEEDS[5]

As we mentioned in the first chapter, we all have unique emotional needs, and certain needs that we all have in common. When you feel a lack of one of these needs in your life, the pursuit of that missing need can become an obsession until you obtain the object of your desires. Similar to an addiction, the mind alone decides what your emotional needs are. We may not even notice when an emotional need is met or not by our spouse or another; it may just be felt in the change of our mood. If the need is being met, we are generally find ourselves in a kinder and more loving energy. If a need goes unfulfilled long enough, however, we may get moody, angry and inadvertently punish our partner. Worse yet, if your partner holds an emotional need hostage in exchange for one of their needs, another downward spiral occurs.

When we fail to bond with our partner, several of our primary emotional needs are most likely not being met. The downward vortex of unmet needs spirals down quickly:

➢ First we protest that we are lacking such needs.

➢ We next become depressed and despair over our unanswered need for a relationship.

➢ Finally, we detach altogether from others and those of the outside world that have so wronged us by not being there for us.

Living with unmet needs is akin to living by yourself on a deserted island. At first you scream at the pirates that left you there, but after a while you get used to it and become that raving

---

[5]Dr. Wilard F. Harley, His Needs Her Needs

guy with the long hair chasing everyone off *his* island. You've forgotten what it is that you've been missing.

A major event that interrupts our emotional needs is the arrival of a child (or 2 or 3 or more!). Visualize the fulfillment of our emotional needs as putting coins in a love bank. You ask your partner about thier day, listen to them talk about their friends, and another coin goes in the bank. You have a nice dinner, romance is in the air, you profess your love…and add another coin.

What happens when a child or two comes along? At a time when a couple is supposed to be truly together, instead of the woman's attention being 100% on her man, it's now split, often in a hugely unbalanced manner. The child is number one. The husband is not being doted over all the time, sex is out the window, no time to be together as a couple, and fewer coins go into the love bank. Suddenly, half of your emotional needs are no longer being met. The wife becomes a mother and a sex-starved dad tries to tough it out and ignore his needs.

The more the husband feigns strength ("It's okay…our child should come first. I'm OK."), the more he is telling himself a lie. Face it; new moms are tired…very tired. After taking care of a newborn and possibly work, the energy necessary to maintain, let alone build, a romantic marital relationship is exceedingly difficult. Without a deep awareness of each other's needs and a few "break from baby" moments, many couples spiral down into roommate status over the years. The emphasis and time was heavily invested in the children and not in the marriage.

Most couples look forward to having a family, but there is no escaping life. The solution is to remember to be there for one another, to communicate, and that there are *two* people in this relationship that need caring for, and both have their own emotional needs. Strong families begin with a strong leadership bond between the parents. An unbalanced focus on the children, work, or any other commitment puts the foundation of the home at risk. You need to remember that without a loving committed couple at the core of it, there *is* no family.

We outlined the 10 emotional needs in the first chapter. Now it's time to fully explore these 10 emotional needs in more detail and find out how their absence can make us go from love to lack.

Admiration:

If you have a strong need for admiration, you may have fallen in love with your spouse partly because of the way he or she compliments or appreciates you. Criticism from your spouse can hurt you deeply if you have this need. All it takes from your partner to fix address this is a few words of admiration.

No one gets together with his or her partner with the expectation of being ignored. There was something about you that she admired, just as there is something about her that you admire. It could have been your intellect, the way you do certain things, the way you pursue your objectives, or even that dreamer's look in your eye. Whatever it was, it helped you win the love lottery early on.

Shame, blame, disrespect, betrayal, and the withholding of affection damage the roots from which love grows. Love can only survive these injuries if they are acknowledged, healed and rare."

But admiration is a hungry beast; just because she said it once to you does not mean it lasts forever. No one goes out of their way to say, "I *don't* admire you," they may simply stop giving out the compliments. As such, any stoppage in the flow of praise can be taken as a sign of having lost the admiration of the other. We need reminders, even if it is the occasional, "Have I ever told you how much I like the way you smile?"

Occasional reminders of one's continued admiration for the other can take the sting out of criticisms that could otherwise deeply hurt a person. This is, after all, the one you love and trust the most, so we be especially sensitive to your partner's need for admiration.

Give it to get it.

Family Commitment:

Besides the greater need for income and responsibilities, the arrival of children creates a new role for both of you in your children's development. You instantly have a family commitment you did not have before the kids arrived. Your need to teach them, spend quality time with them, and see that they turn out as caring, successful people reshapes who you are and what you do on a daily basis.

Problems arise if the methods for rearing your children are in conflict with what your spouse's values. If your spouse does not meet the standards and methods you so enthusiastically approve, then you may feel that your spouse is neglecting your children. When your spouse's participation in family activities meets your goals and future for your children, your love for your partner will increase, depositing a flood of coins into your love bank.

Make sure the domestic goals of you and your partner are in sync with one another. If they are not, the two of you need to talk. Come to some basic agreements before family roles and responsibilities become part of your lifestyle. How do the two of you want to raise the children? How do you want to discipline them? Discuss these issues early, before it's critical. If the kids are already here, it's not too late. Set aside some ground rules on how to make a fresh start.

1. Leave past successes and failures off the table.
2. Read a book or take a course together on parenting.
3. Explore strategies and tactics in child rearing one idea at a time.
4. Study successsful parents and get input on what they do.
5. If the kids are older, get their 'buy in' too.

Affection:

Affection is the expression of care; a symbol of security, comfort, and approval. Affection tells the other person how important he or she is to you and shows, by example, how concerned you are with their problems. Affection can be expressed with a simple hug, or a greeting card that says, "I love you" delivered for no reason other than that you do. It's not a holiday, and it's not a "get out of the doghouse" moment; you simply love her. You show affection because:

1) you want to show it, and

2) your partner wants to receive it.

Holding hands, a walk after dinner, back rubs, and so forth, are simple gestures that go a long way for a person with a strong emotional need of affection. When the simple acts of affection are unashamedly and freely given, they cement a relationship.

The lack of affection, conversely can whittle away your bond.

When a child is born, in the process of showing affection to this new life, one often forgest the one who helped you create this new life still needs some affection as well. Take consistent time and continue to show affection for one another. Even a brief kiss, a touch, or a word can do wonders.

Sexual Fulfillment:

You and your spouse promised to be faithful to one another, to be each other's only sexual partner for life. You trusted one another to meet your sexual needs, be available and responsive. If you have this need then you are solely dependent upon your spouse to see them fulfilled. In most cultures, there is no other ethical choice.

A sexual need can be different from wanting to make love with your spouse. You want to make love with your partner as a reflection of the deep emotional need you have for that person, but a purely sexual need can predate you're ever having met. It is a need that can now only be met by your partner, and if it is not met, people often look outside of their marriage to have that need met.

Sex works on more than one level, but at its most basic level, sexual desires are imprinted on humans to propagate the species. It is a chemical desire that remains strong with adults well past the point of being able to bear children. Problems arise when, as is true in many cases, the sex drive of a couple is not in balance.

There are scores of books written on sex, sexuality and intimacy. For a recommended list, visit our resource section at www.relationshipsociety.com.

Conversation:

Conversation is not a need that can always be met exclusively in the bonds of a marriage. We have the need to connect with other people, as well as our mate. However, whoever meets that need best will be depositing more coins into your love bank. Be very wary of your emotional needs being met outside of your marriage. When a spouse isn't depositing enough coins in that bank, other players may enter the picture to fill that need.

This can easily become an emotional affair.

Emotional affairs can often turn into sexual affairs, but at the core both are the result of unmet needs. Healthy, consistent, vibrant conversation can stave off one person's need to seek connection outside of your monogamous relationship.

Conversation is more than simply talking. Active listening is vital to making sure deposits into your love bank aren't counterfeit! It is a mutual exchange on topics of common interest that fulfills the following requirements:

➢ All participants have an equal opportunity to speak.

➢ The speaker of the moment has the undivided attention of the others involved in the conversation.

➢ The conversation is enjoyable by both parties.

The needs of good conversation are *not* met, however, if any of the following occurs:

➢ Disrespect is shown.

➢ Demands are made.

➢ Someone becomes angry.

➢ The opportunity is used to dwell on past mistakes.

If inauthentic conversation happens, the couple is better off not talking to one another at all. An unpleasant conversation only ensures there will be less opportunity to meet this need in the future.

After marriage, some women find their man's interest in talking to them wane a bit. If the need for conversation was fulfilled during courtship, then it is reasonable to assume that the partner assumes this fulfillment will continue. If one of the reasons you fell in love was because of the way you could talk with her, a lack of that need will raise the risk of falling out of love.

"We need to talk," however, is not the best way to initiate or rekindle that part of your relationship! Instead of forcing the idea of conversation upon a withdrawer, ask a question, start a topic, tell a joke, or share a story. Let it flow naturally. The art of conversation becomes more difficult as we become intimately familiar with our partner.

If you enjoy conversation just to talk with someone, beyond the practical means to an end, and become frustrated when you have not been able to talk to someone for a while, then conversation is one of your most important emotional needs.

Let your partner know.

Honesty and Openness:
Most people want an honest relationship with their spouse, but some people have a particular need for honesty and openness at any cost. People with a high need for honesty feel secure and emotionally bonded when that need is fully met. Those with this need want accurate information on their spouse's thoughts, feelings, likes, activities, and plans, regardless of what it may mean. Without this level of untarnished honesty, trust is

Non-judgmental Honesty

IIn order for two people to be 100% honest, some rules are in order. On one hand, if a person values honesty but then berates or is hurt by an honest comment, they are not creating an environment for honesty.

A person who values honesty must be disconnected from the outcome. An environment of honesty is non-judgmental and free from retaliation.

Suppose "Bob" tells "Linda" that he's not comfortable with her wearing a particular blouse because it is overly revealing. If Linda accuses Bob of being jealous or paranoid, she is not establishing a safe environment for Bob to be honest.

She may still want to wear the blouse, but if she doesn't respect Bob's feelings, he may be reluctant to be honest in the future.

undermined, insecurity can develop, and the person questions the very foundation of the relationship.

When you and your spouse openly share your past, present, future hopes and dreams, then you can make intelligent decisions that take one another's feelings into account. You feel good about yourself and the relationship. You appreciate it when your spouse reveals their most private thoughts to you. If, on the other hand, you feel they are keeping secrets from you, this can engender feelings of paranoia and distrust. If this is the case, then you have an emotional need for honesty and openness.

Ideally, if you value this need, you must be able to separate honesty from emotion. It is only when you can fully disconnect from the outcome, that one's need for honesty can be completely satisfied.

Recreational Companionship:

Before marriage, you probably planned your dates around your favorite recreational activities. When this is an important emotional need for you, recreational companionship can drop a few pounds of those love coins into your bank. To get your relationship to flourish, chose activities you both enjoy. Don't make the mistake of doing only whatever the one with the greatest need wants to do.

Serving a social need separately can cause the couple to go their separate ways. If the husband joins his friends in his favorite activities, while the wife goes about enjoying her own separate activities by herself, a need is being met, but add to that activities you both enjoy.

By engaging in your own favorite activities, *someone* is going to be putting love coins into your bank. Wouldn't it be best if it was your spouse making all these deposits? A couple should be one another's favorite recreational companion.

Recreational companionship actually combines two needs:

1) The need to be engaged in a recreational activity.

2) The need to have a companion to enjoy it with.

If you crave a certain activity, and require a companion for fulfillment, then you need to include recreational companionship in your list of emotional needs.

This particular emotion need ties into honesty as well. A relationship begins during courting and continues into marriage. When you start sharing recreational activities, be honest from the very beginning what you do and don't like to do. Saying you "like" an activity during courting just to get closer will come back to hurt you after marriage; you'll stop doing things together because you've discovered there was nothing you really liked doing together in the first place.

If you are already in a committed relationship, don't despair. Use this knowledge to try new things! People change, situations morph, and you may both discover a new activity you had previously ignored.

Physical Attractiveness:

Let's face it; the first thing that draws most couples to one another is physical attractiveness. We instantly judge and are attracted to specific attributes that turn us on. It could be your partner's hair or even the shape of a leg.

Everyone has their own view of beauty, but the basics are however he or she looked when they courted, is most likely the standard set for the marriage. Many a complaint in a marriage revolves around the spouse losing their attractiveness, gaining weight, or not taking the time to look good. The entrance of a child into the relationship is a common cause; so busy with being a mother, the woman forgets that she is also a wife. She becomes a sweat suit house bunny, then wonders why the husband has stopped complimenting her. Or the husband, so obsessed with earning a proper living for his growing family, lets himself go, watches his waistline grow, and cares less and less about remaining that attractive young man that he used to be.

The result can be frustration, disrespectful tones, impatience, and things not getting done. You grow apart, and your argumentativeness reduces what attractive qualities are left. You've lost respect for your spouse, and yourself as well.

A quick look in the mirror and a sincere focus on your OWN self-esteem is the starting point. Commit to proper nutrition and fitness, and interest about how you dress and look. Beauty is in the eye of the beholder, but if what you are beholding is important, make sure your spouse knows and add this to your list of emotional needs.

Financial Support:

Some people marry not specifically for money, but for financial security. Others marry before the subject of financial security becomes important. When a life-changing event pops up, (a spouse becomes unemployed) and the household income drops, it becomes a consideration to be faced. Whatever the reason, money *can* influence your relationship and spill over into how you treat each other.

Couples have different views of what constitutes good financial support. Is it good enough to simply get by, or do you have larger goals to aspire to? The same couple may have different answers at different stages in their lives as their needs change.

Many couples have traced the cause of their disputes down to arguing about finances. Couples with secure connections find themselves working on the problem as a team instead of working against one another.

- If a person were to meet your financial needs would they be easier to fall in love with?
- Does a person's wealth make him more attractive?
- If he were poor and unemployable and told you that you would have to support the both of you, would you still fall in love?

If you find that money will influence your final decision, then you have a need for financial support. Does this sound shallow? Drop the judgement, finances are one of the foundational components for security and the core human need of certainty.

Domestic Support:

In our modern times this one seems a bit old fashioned, yet it exists in the back of every relationship. In days past, it used to be the husband that worked, and the wife that kept the home fires burning. Cooking meals, washing dishes, cleaning house, and childcare were roles that predominantly went to the wife.

Times have changed.

Nowadays many women work, have careers, and gain some pleasure from the man contributing to a well-managed home. In many Western cultures, most marriages begin with both spouses willing to share the load of domestic responsibilities, dividing the household chores between them. For the first time the groom gets some help with chores he's had to do all by himself, and the wife is glad that she's not there solely as an indentured servant. Domestic support is not yet seen as an emotional support.

Then the children arrive on the scene.

Children create a lot of needs; financial and domestic, and the old division of labor often goes out the window. Both spouses must share a new set of responsibilities, but who will take the lead? This is when you discover if domestic support is strong issue with either of you. When your circumstances change and a greater need arises that throws off the previous plan, it's time to discuss a new division of labor, and be ready to make on-the-spot adjustments to your well-oiled machine.

If you find yourself very appreciative of your spouse's cooking, cleaning, and childcare, and are frustrated when it's not there, rate domestic support as an emotional need. Then talk about it.

From Savannah:

We had a couple that had moved from Utah to Las Vegas. They had been married for thirty years, both very senior in their companies they worked for. The wife discovered that her husband had an affair whenever he traveled to and from Utah and some other places. She found out that it was an affair with another man because the boyfriend was angry he wasn't spending enough time with him.

Needless to say she was shocked, and when asked what she felt really went wrong, she said, *"Well, we are both traveling so much, but we have this nice home life, like we are best friends. He has been my best friend this whole time. We had a child together."*

So I asked, *"Well, what about sex?"*

Her reply was that sex had never really been up there, and that he was her first. For his generation it was not okay to simply come out and be gay and still be successful, so he had an affair. Once this surfaced, the affair was ended, and the husband announced that he wanted his married relationship more than being homosexual, so he said that he would try.

Will he be able to be faithful in a marriage with a heterosexual wife? When I asked the wife, she paused a moment and thought about it. Her answer was insightfully honest. "It doesn't really matter. We have this tight bond for thirty years. With this new discovery, we actually became closer as a couple." Our coaching sessions were thoroughly transformative…they both reconnected at a new and deeper level.

We rebooted their relationship.

We compartmentalized their needs as individuals, who he is, who she is, and what they are willing to accept. It was not about traditional marriage, or dating, or being gay, but about the relationship of two individuals, regardless of how it began.

Be clear about what you want, communicate openly with your partner, and let them be open with you. If you want your love to not just survive but thrive, ask yourself a couple of questions.

> ➢ Does your relationship fulfill your emotional needs now and in the future?
> ➢ Does it have the potential to fulfill your needs?
> ➢ Do you believe it is something worth fighting for?

However you begin, however you change over the years, be aware that you and your spouse each have emotional needs. Be sensitive to them, communicate any changes in your needs, and listen to what the other says.

Communicate.

BARRIERS TO LOVE: THE LOVE KILLERS

Despite our best efforts and our fanciful dreams, it seems most relationships fail catastrophically or like a cancer, die painfully and quietly.

Why?

There are many barriers to a deep, connected love; poisons within our beliefs and communication that infect our relationships. It is imperative to look within ourselves and understand the barriers we have, ourselves, erected in our hearts. Becoming aware of our own barriers is step #1 to quickly and permanently removing them so we can connect easily and lovingly in the future.

Below are nine love killers that you need to watch out for:

- Self-Centeredness
- Lack of Observing Oneself
- Inability to Validate Another
- Playing Fair
- Emotional Detachment
- Control and Denial Separateness
- The Wish For Eden
- Parental Dynamics
- Lack of Boundaries

Self-Centeredness:

Self-Centeredness can be defined as a person who experiences life mostly in terms of his or her self. The self-centered person believes their life exists to make him happy. Others are there only as extensions of himself. The truly selfish person views any event in terms of how it affects himself alone. A self-centered person guarantees the failure of love or any sort of love-based attachment by denying the reality of anyone else; he can never adapt himself to another's needs or wishes. He is narcissistic, with an inability to process shame or compassion, and is unable to sacrifice himself for the needs of another unless he gets something in return that better benefits him.

It often begins as manipulation. They get what they want and see only the reward without the sacrifice that others may have made to make it so. Soon, it becomes a habit, the expectation that this is the way the world works and it works around him alone. No meaningful relationship can endure based on one person.

To consider persons and events and situations only in the light of their effect upon myself is to live on the doorstep of hell"

-Thomas Merton

The truly self-centered person can never have any sort of deep relationship, as the very concept implies *two* people, and from his or her point of view there is only the one.

Lack of Observing Oneself:
One of the most frustrating qualities one can have is the inability to see one's self as others might, to look in the mirror and not see what looks back. Like the person who's on the dance floor, "boogying down," moon walking, and dancing so very fine, when in reality he's just shaking a little and nodding his head. No one is perfect, and most people freely admit that, but the way towards fixing our problems and improving ourselves lies in our ability to clearly see our problems in the first place.

Someone in a relationship gets injured by some fault of the other, only the other sees no fault within himself, never apologizes, never sets things straight since there is nothing to correct.

The relationship gets stuck. That bad dancer on the dance floor is never going to take dance lessons if he thinks his every move is like Fred Astaire. No conflict can be resolved until the one person admits to himself that he has a problem.

Take a good long look at yourself and be brutally honest. Are you really the best dancer on the floor? Are you really that cool dude with nothing to worry about? No one is perfect, no one without fault, and that includes you. Assume that you aren't the Fred Astaire of relationships and there is room for improvement.

Only then can you truly groove to the beat of a great relationship.

Inability to Validate Another:

One of our deepest needs is to be understood and validated by others. We don't necessarily have to be told that we're right all the time, just see that someone understands how we feel and where we are coming from. When we are upset or feel a certain way, then we need to know others understand our needs. Emotional disaster can strike when we are dismissed out of hand. Being invalidated is like a child being told Santa Claus doesn't exist.

When we get hurt, no one wants to hear, "Oh come on now, that didn't hurt." Isn't it nicer to hear, "Hey, are you alright? That sounded like a difficult experience for you." The latter builds connections between people, while the former breaks them.

A key component to validating someone is empathy. Don't confuse sympathy with empathy. Empathy is the ability to feel how a person feels, listen to their words and hear the pain or joy behind them. Empathy creates a connection as it permits you to feel what is troubling the other person. When we can feel their emotions, an instant connection results. The antithesis, indifference is baffling. If you have ever heard, "You don't get me, you never understood me?" the connection isn't present and the empathetic feeling is missing.

There was a man at one of our seminars, Mike, and he was leaving the seminar early. When I asked why, he said he was going to see his wife's art exhibit. He didn't love art, in fact hated it, but he loved to see the way his wife looks when she's doing what she loves to do; the look in her eyes, her body language. He loved to see her come alive at her art exhibits, and so he would attend as well. Rather than simply blowing it off as just "her thing", he validated her in her choice of passion, and that only strengthened their love of one another.

Validation doesn't even have to be dramatic. Is your partner a good cook? Tell them. Great with the kids? Say something. It could be anything from supporting their passion and life's ambition to remarking on a recent acheivement at work or home.

Another couple was attending a seminar together and the wife was supposed to drive to Palm Springs to pick up the kids then meet her hubby later. When he suggested this "driving separately" scenario, a panic attack bubbled up within her. She wondered if she'd find a gas station or get lost. Her husband instantly recognized her high state of anxiety and made the decision to go with her rearrange the kid/business pick up schedule. The relief that flooded through her was visible; she could breathe again. You may not always be able to adapt your schedule to meet the emotional needs of your partner, but acknowledging the need and offering a solution will get you more than half way there.

Sometimes all it takes is to say, "I understand," and mean it.

Playing Fair:

We treat others as they treat us. If they are good to us, we are good to them. Does this also means that if they are bad to us then we are bad to them? No one is good all the time; there are times when there is poor behavior in a relationship. Do we return maliciously or inadvertently return more bad behavior?

That is why this "fairness" does not always work. We cannot sink to the worst possible behavior in a relationship, rather, we should rise above it gracefully in spite of any occasional slights. It's like the difference between the Old and New Testaments; "eye for an eye" became "turn the other cheek."

Don't retaliate on bad behavior. Lead with good behavior. When you treat others the way you wish to be treated, you might not always get a reciprocal response, but you'll certainly receive more good than bad. The golden rule works.

Emotional Unattachment:

Uncontrolled empathy can affect the receiver negatively if done without unattachment. A highly empathetic person often absorbs a person's plight and sadness to the point where they cannot separate their feelings from their partner. When you are be empathetic, but unattached from their energy, you can connect with them while protecting yourself. Being **de**tached from emotions can come off as a bit frosty; even cold. Without an empathetic underpinning, emotional detachment will not work.

Being unattached from an outcome (or from the result of being honest) however, is a different manner. You can love unconditionally, be fully present, empathetic and still be **un**attached from the outcome. Being unattached is different than being detached.

❖ When you are unattached, you are open, honest and loving, but not committed to an outcome (which you may have no control of anyway).

❖ When you are detached, you are aloof and uncaring.

Control and Denial Separateness:

Freedom is important especially with married couples. Sure, you two are "one", but to deny them their freedom to also be an individual, and they may decide to separate emotionally, physically or completely. Some people see their partners solely as extensions of themselves. The reality, however, is when there is a "We" there are always two "I's." Those who attempt to control the freedom of the one they love may only be loving themselves and will end up with just themselves.

This is a dangerous program that needs a delicate balance.

Love can only exist where there is freedom. When someone says "No," one must learn to respect the statement, for that is showing how you respect the person. And if you didn't really respect your partner, then your relationship may not be built on solid ground. If your partner needs his space, give it, because only then will you know he will always return and be there for you.

While we've mentioned the coins as deposits, Love itself is not a currency that can be taken and "saved." Love only works when it is given freely. It has been said in many ways before, that the tighter you try to grip something, the more it will slip through your fingers. Love is something gentle that can be crushed by not enough care and also lost to too tight a grip. The old saying about letting a butterfly go and having it come back if it loves you is cute…and true.

The Wish For Eden:

We live in an imperfect world. We may strive for perfection, but perfection is a goal, not a reality. People have flaws that cannot always be "fixed." Some people have a perfect image in their minds of either who they want to be with or the person they are with right now. When that perfect image clashes with the reality of the occasional flaw here and there, trouble ensues. People change. People grow. New patterns emerge.

There is no 100% ideal, perfect match.

Refering back to wabi-sabi love and embrace the little imperfections in your love instead of becoming annoyed by them. If you keep focusing on the flaws, they will become bigger and more pronounced in your eyes until they become unbearable. Like looking at life through a magnifying lens, that which we focus on becomes larger. That distant crack becomes a valley, and that odd way she sets the table becomes a National news item. The bigger a deal you make of a small imperfection, the more the other person will defend it, until the gulf that separates you becomes insurmountable.

Parental Dynamics:

The parent-child dynamic should never be emulated between a loving couple. Adults are supposed to know better than the child, and adult communication should be give and take, as opposed to "Do as I say."

This need for domineering control, to have the other be subject to them, bears less a resemblance to a loving relationship and more a resemblance to teaching a toddler basic manners. There is no gender bias on Parental Dynamics. Husbands and wives are equally guilty of talking down to their partners.

In either case, one person feels like a victim.

Truth is, there is no one holding a gun to your head, no legal document that says you have no will of your own. Tell your partner how you feel and why. Realize in the end you are always your own person. You are only under another's control when you *allow* the other person to control you. Only an unattached, non-judgmental and honest discussion will empower both parties to become equal partners.

Be truthful and transparent. Be honest with your partner so they do not feel the need to control every aspect around themselves. If one "insists" that you be home by a certain time, calmly say, "I have a business meeting tonight; it should be done by eight." Then it's up to the other person to listen and understand. Conversely, if there is a way you can reschedule the meeting to meet your partner's needs and be home at a certain time-do it.

A disempowering coping strategy is the silent treatment. It doesn't work with children, and is certainly not going to work with adults. Neither will the threat of withholding sex. All any of that will do is make matters worse, engendering feelings of alienation and anger. Any method of attempting to control behavior as opposed to encouraging behavior will fail, long-term.

There is only one method of influence that works.

Unconditional love.

When you love, cherish, accept and are unattached from the outcome of any disagreements, your partner will eventually follow that pattern.

You both win.

Lack Of Boundaries:

Our last love killer is boundaries, or a lack thereof. A Lack of Boundries example would be when someone says "No" and you fail to have the proper reaction to it. Boundary problems arise from an inability to either say or hear the word "No". If we allow someone to walk over us in a way that destroys respect, or we walk all over him without caring, a boundry is crossed. True love respects boundaries; we need to respect it when we hear that word "no", and learn to say it when we need to.

A boundary may be physical, emotional, spiritual, sexual, or relational. Your personal boundries may need to be discussed openly with your partner. Oftentimes, they may not be aware of what's going on in your head. If you step on someone's toes on the dance floor too often and you may lose your dance partner. If you fail to explain your boundries, "Hey, you're stepping on my feet," you'll soon have sore feet.

Too much treading upon another's boundaries also creates a feeling of loss of self, and this can lead to distraction and a breakdown in the relationship. The person whose boundries are bing violated might employ a negative coping strategy, such as drinking.

Love means respect, and respect means listening. When you hear, "I love you, but I still have to say no," you've opened your heart, but kept your boundaries. A balanced relationship never suffers from this style of communication.

Sometimes a boundary lies not within yourself, but something very destructive within your partner. An extreme example would be a drug addiction. Presenting this boundary in a way that points out the problem without bringing offense will help allow the person to save face. "I love you and it hurts me so much to see you abuse yourself. Can we talk about getting you help, please?"

Even a small boundary may grow into a larger issue, so be clear and open, but take action. Hesitation and hoping the boundary will change rarely works. Take care to erect your boundaries against not only whatever would threaten your own individuality, but your relationship.

The slope from Love to Lack is slippery, that dance floor beneath your feet waxed to a fine polish. It takes some work to keep your footing, an eye open for the stumbling blocks that may lie in your path, but in the end the dance is well worth the effort.

Chapter Three Summary

- Become aware of your Family Origin Issues
- The Relationship Dance- reconnecting after being hurt: Acknowledge, Share, Talk/Touch
- To avoid problems: Believe in your spouse, risk doing things differently, tell your spouse what it is about her/him that you love.
- The 10 Emotional Needs: Admiration, Family Commitment, Affection, Sexual Fulfillment, Conversation, Recreational Companionship, Honesty and Openness, Physical Attractiveness, Financial Support, Domestic Support
- Love Killers: self-centeredness, lack of observing oneself, inability to validate another, playing fair, emotional detachment, control and denial separateness, the wish for Eden, parental dynamics, lack of boundaries.

Chapter Four:

STEP 1:
FIXING IT- START WITH "I"

"Be the change you want to see in the world."
-Ghandi

For a thorough cleaning of your relationship hard drive, nothing beats a system upgrade and a fresh software install. With a thorough understanding of your personality, history and the manner in which you seek and express love, it becomes easier to become a better partner in the "We" part of your relationship. The three-step process we'll outline in the next few chapters covers the basics.

Our WE³ experiential retreats are designed to make the changes seamless, fun and permanent. For the purposes of this book, however, we want to outline the tools you'll need to do as much of this work on your own.

The first step to fixing a relationship is to fix the individuals within it. Your "We" has two "I's" within it, the foundation of the "We", so it makes sense to first fix the foundation that supports the relationship.

Just as in a dance, before you go back out to that dance floor to boogey with your chosen partner, set some time aside to learn the steps yourself.

Awareness

Everyone has his or her own baggage going into a relationship. That's not a judgment, it is simply part of being a human being in society. Becoming aware and being 100% honest about your baggage is the hardest, but essential first step. Your baggage may be heavy or light, multiple cases or a single bag. Your baggage may be old or new, but we all have it. Take a moment and ignore your partner's baggage. Your first step is to unlock your own.

"Love is not something we give or get; it is something that we nurture and grow, a connection that can only be cultivated between two people when it exists within each one of them- we can only love others as much as we love ourselves."

Describing your baggage comes with an initial discussion of becoming fully aware of your self, strengths, and limitations. Become aware of your own limitations, quirks, and desires so they don't sneak up and surprise you and your partner later on in the relationship. What happened in your past to create your belief system? What relationship in the past caused you to decrease your trust? The list is as endless as lines of code in a program.

Here is a great example:

Bill C. and Sara, came to our clinic recently. Bill had sold his business that year for 25 million dollars. Even though Bill had sold his business, he was retained for 2 years during the transition. He had more time to spend with Sara and connect with her, but Bill was still fully responsible for the success of the business.

Even with the extra time they both had, Sara could not connect with Bill. When Bill was working 7 days a week, there was a tacit understanding that it was okay for her to get her "connection time" outside of her marriage. Unfortunately, she connected wonderfully with someone Bill had been doing business with for quite a while. There was no sexual activity, but plenty of flirting

An emotional affair was in full swing.

The affair was enough, however, to affect the Bill's business. "If I can't trust him with my wife, I'll be damned if I'd trust him with my clients," he blurted out during one of our sessions.

For Bill and Sara, the real issue wasn't a lack of connection, but a lack of empathy. They couldn't connect with each other because of a host of poor attachment styles, over-stepping boundries and vulnerability issues. I told him that even though she is in the wrong, he is overly guarded and that created a real lack of empathy for his wife.

He is a successful businessman, a leader. Outwardly, he appeared to be controlling, a statement which his wife agreed with.

He was not overly controlling; he had very firm boundaries which, because of his lack of empathy, showed up as being very controlling to her. The area he needed to improve upon was empathy.

Once we opened up and brought to the surface his power to change himself, he was able to create sincere empathy for his wife and her needs for an emotional connection outside of the marriage faded away. The emotional affair ended, the business transition went well and Bill and Sara reconnected securely.

The marriage was saved.

Subsequent to this rapid discovery, we looked into other issues, such as control being an illusion. No one controls you, you *give* someone control over you, just as the wife gave up control of her life to her husband. Except for the case of an extreme narcissist, there is no real control being attempted or implied. Issues such as lack of empathy lead to a lack of respect, which leads the partner to assume there is a control problem. However, the real problem lies in awareness; of what you need as an "I".

Bill realized he needed to bring down some of his protection mechanisms so he can be more empathetic and understanding towards his wife moving forward. They are living this luxurious lifestyle, but money can't purchase secure connection.

In the case of this couple, they have all the money they could need or want, but all she needed was a friend and partner.

Start by looking deep within to find the "I" within you, the individual.

❖ What is your attachment style?

❖ Your founding relationships in life?

❖ How secure were you with your parents?

Begin with questions like those, and then look at your boundaries.

In the story above, the stated issue was control, but by using our WE³ methodology, we found out more…much more.

The history of the Bill and Sara created beliefs that needed to be addressed. For one, they met when she had just come out of a divorce and he was still married. The first eight years of their relationship was while he was married. Upon reflection, both parties saw that many of her issues developed around those experiences; she was the mistress waiting patiently in the corner. If it could happen to her as a mistress, would it happen to her as the wife?

They were in a fantasy relationship for most of their time together, eight years of fun and only three years of living together in normal day-to-day life. It was a ten-year honeymoon period that only now are they getting over. It took over 10 years to deal with each other's problems, boundaries, and realities. He had to learn how to be vulnerable enough with her to be empathetic and communicate on the level that they should be doing so as spouses.

This is a perfect example of working on the "I" to get to the "We". To fix this relationship, Bill needed to fix his issues as much as Sara did. They needed to become aware of their connection styles and needs. To help any couple visualize what they need to work on, we draw a nest of triangles. Each triangle within this figure represents one of the barriers that must be overcome to achieve real intimacy. Attachment, Boundaries, Trust, Safety, Vulnerability, and Intimacy. This six-sided construct allows any couple to being looking at any area of themselves in order to become more aware of how they connect, communicate and attach. You can pick any one of these areas to do a little discovery about who you are and why you are.

We use a sexagon (no pun intended) instead of a ladder because there is no set order that you have to achieve each of these goals.

THE INTIMACY SEXAGON

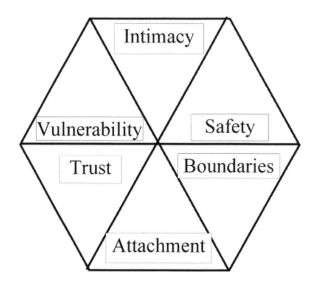

Attachment:

We covered the basic attachment styles in an earlier chapter; this is merely the graphical depiction of what may have to be worked on in that department. Is your partner's attachment style conducive to a solid relationship or is there room for them (and you) for improvement?

Boundaries:

Boundaries are the rules by which you engage with other people. In our earlier story Sara was emotionally attached to Bill's business partner, but the business partner didn't realize he was having an emotional affair. Was it was okay for her to keep that relationship going. "No. There is no way," Bill stated emphatically. This was his boundary, and it also echoes our first rule for healing a relationship: any affairs must end before a trust and connection can occur in your partnership.

Trust:

Do you trust each other? If you believe people are inherently good, trusting is easier. Many people have trust "issues" where a betrayal in a past relationship pollutes ones' ability to trust in a new relationship. if you are constantly questioning your partner, your ability to develop a secure connection is impossible? Trust is a deep knowing the other person will abide by your boundries.

Safety:

Can I count on you? In our earlier example, Bill had twenty-five million reasons to feel secure, but to Sara, this was not the currency she valued. She access to financial security was way down the list of her needs. Sara's ability to feel safe, her currency of choice was conversation and communication.

Vulnerability:

As mentioned earlier in this book, before you can develop trust, one must be vulnerable. When you drop your armor and open yourself to potential ridicule, your are vulnerable. Will your parnter shoot or put down their weapon? When you confide in your partner, you trust they will not exploit your perceived weakness. When you open yourself up, you are trusting your partner to do the same. Vulnerability leads to trust and trust creates security. When these three items fall into place, your intimacy has the potential to deepen.

Intimacy:

Intimacy can be expressed emotionally, spiritually and physically. A great way to measure and explore your intimacy is to remember the acroynm E.S.P. Complete intimacy is a combination of these three styles of connection:

- Emotional
- Spiritual
- Physical

Besides having a great easy-to-remember acronym, intimacy is at the top of the pyramid in developing a secure and loving connection with your partner. Your understanding of one another becomes intuitive. Early on in your growth cycles, you will have to share openly, ask questions, make mistakes and exercise your trust muscles to develop a secure connection.

Once you develop these muscles to the point where they are a habit, your intimacy naturally deepens. You are two "I's" that have become a "WE". Your dance of intimacy is effortless as you float through you're your challenges and successes as a couple.

DISCOVERING YOUR SOLUTION[6]

Emotional intelligence allows you to become aware of who you are and how you impact others. How do you "show up" in a relationship? To fix the problem within yourself that prevents intimacy, one must become self-aware. Facing your own faults isn't easy. It requires courage. Courage to be vulnerable, face your imperfections, and have compassion for yourself. Developing an authentic ability to be self aware requires you to see yourself the way other people see you. If you're in a disconnected relationship, repairing it is not a solo job; you cannot do it alone.

---

[6] Dan Spiegel, The Developing Mind and Dan Goldman, Emotional intelligence

You will need unfiltered feedback from others.

This level of healing must be done in a trusted relationship. Moreover, your trusted confidant must also be 100% honest with you. Many couples start with a counselor, coach or therapist to begin this discussion. Ultimately, you'll want to develop enough trust and non-judgemental communication with your partner for this, as they probably know you the best.

Your ability to be self-aware will take a bit of mediation, awkward questions and non-judgmental discovery. But, when you own up to who you are, you will be able to become a better "I" that can more securely become part of a "We".

With the proper attitude, patience and commitment to become a better "I", your "We" will blossom and strengthen.

Let's get started.

Chapter Four Summary

- Awareness: Have a full awareness of self
- The Intimacy sexagon: Attachment, Trust, Boundaries, Vulnerability, Safety, and Intimacy
- Imprints from our past: Be aware of using past events as excuses for continuing current undesirable behaviors and actions.
- Emotional intelligence is about becoming more aware of who you are and how you impact others.
- Healing your psyche and your self cannot be done alone.

Chapter Five:

STEP 2:
FROM "I" TO "WE"

"You can't practice relating.
You can only be related."

We drawn th analogy that relationships are similar to computers. When either are running smoothly it is a thing of beauty, but when there's a glitch, it becomes frustrating beyond belief. In the previous chapter we discussed glitches that develop from the individual, the "I" in the relationship, how to spot and repair them. Now, much like for a computer program, we can reboot the relationship; and apply the new program to the computer's system; the "We."

The process of this reboot is not as simple as just flipping a switch. Between the "I" and the "We" there is the journey that gets us from one to the other, the process of belonging with another person. Like many journeys, there is a right way and a wrong way to approach it, a safe path and a dangerous path. We'll point you along the correct path, and assist you in rebooting your relationship so that the two of you can go sliding smoothly across your relationship dance floor with laughter and love.

GET PAST DENIAL

Since it is impossible to change another person; we can only ourselves, we started with the "I". It is a psychotherapist's job to help people look beyond their denials, examine childhood issues, discover connection styles and communicate boundries with their partner. Before anyone can repair what's broken, you first have to know what is broken.

From Savannah:

I had a couple, Frank and Janet. Frank had an affair two years prior before coming into counseling. From the beginning, his attitude towards that event was, *"It's been two years, get over it. Ancient history. Nothing wrong with me; we've been married twenty years so I must have done something right."* I asked him how many of those years, prior to the affair, was he happy. Then I asked Janet how many years had she been happily married. The answers, (surprise!) weren't even close.

They had disconnected to the point where their relationship was more 'roommate' status than husband and wife. Their words were short and sharp, with no feeling. It was like they were both clocking in at an assembly line. They were going through the motions, but neither had any passion for their relationship.

Both had needs, and neither were able to express them openly. In Frank's case, he craved some attention and validation. It was not happening within the bounds of his marriage and it was a core need of his.

He had found it at work.

When I first got them into therapy he was protective and in denial of himself. Frank was beyond disengaged. He wasn't present at all. Emotionally, he was asleep and in need of a bucket of water over his frozen head.

I had to snap him out of it.

"If you are not willing to be real about your feelings, how you treat your wife, and admit how miserable YOU are, then leave the office, Frank. You don't even have to pay for the session, just leave because you'll get no value in your current state," I calmly told him.

The frost on his deameanor, melted away within seconds.

He sighed, *"Ok…you know, you're right. I am miserable and I don't want to live this way anymore…let's do this."*

He had forgotten how to have a relationship, how to connect because he couldn't be bothered anymore. He had accepted the fact that being miserable and unhappy was normal. The little things like not putting on a clean shirt every day, not kissing his wife in the morning or touching her arm, or giving her a back rub were gone. It was all a non-event. He soon realized he was miserable, and that was the reason the affair happened. As soon as someone else gave him some attention, he went for it. He wasn't in love with his

We cultivate love when we allow our most vulnerable and powerful selves to be deeply seen and known, and when we honor the spiritual connection that grows from that offering with trust, respect, kindness and affection."

mistress or even attracted to her. She merely was a magnet for his unmet needs. This isn't to say his wife was solely responsible for his needs, of course. He needed to clean up his act and she needed to communicate where the soap was.

Their challenges came from a lack of deep, non-judgmental communication. The affair was the symptom. The disease was their mutual disconnection of communication.

It uncomfortable to uncover and admit your failures. When you are blind to the truth and believe your own B.S., sometimes a person needs to face their own lies, altered truths and examine the deep issues within.

We've included our Emotional Needs Questionnaire[7] in this book for you to use. Fill in your answers alone, with no influence from each other, before comparing notes afterwards.

This questionnaire is designed to help you determine your most important emotional needs and evaluate your spouse's effectiveness in meeting those needs. Answer all the questions as candidly as possible. Do not try to minimize any needs that you feel have been unmet.

When you have completed this questionnaire, go through it a second time to be certain your answers accurately reflect your feelings. Do not erase your original answers, but cross them out lightly so that your spouse can see the corrections and discuss them with you.

The final page of this questionnaire asks you to identify and rank five of the ten needs in order of their importance to you. The most important emotional needs are those that give you the most pleasure when met and frustrate you when unmet.

---

[7] Willard Harley, His Needs, Her Needs

Resist the temptation to identify as most important only those needs that your spouse is not presently meeting. Include *all* your emotional needs in your consideration of those that are most important.

Couples who have worked on their "I's" can usually go through their answers together, discussing their responses as a "We."

Ranking Your Emotional Needs
Ten basic emotional needs are listed below. There is also space for you to add other emotional needs that you feel are essential to your marital happiness, but are not included in the list.

In the space provided in front of each need, write a number from 1 to 5 that ranks the need's most importance to your happiness. Write a "1" before the most important need, a "2" before the next most important, and so on until you have ranked all five.

To help you rank these needs, imagine that you will only have one need met in your marriage. Which would make you the happiest, knowing that all the others would go unmet? That need should be "1." If only two needs would be met, what would your second selection be? Which five needs, when met, would make you the happiest.

- o Affection
- o Sexual Fulfillment
- o Conversation
- o Recreational Companionship
- o Honesty and Openness
- o An Attractive Spouse

o Financial Support

o Domestic Support

o Family Commitment

o Admiration

KNOW WHAT YOU DON'T KNOW

The concept of *unconscious incompetence* is best given by the example of a child first learning to tie his shoe. His parents always tied his shoes before, so it was never really something he'd give a thought of. He did not feel powerless because he didn't know there was something he was missing out on; he was *unconsciously incompetent*. One day he sees a friend tying his shoes and he realizes he's missing out, he wants to do it himself. He is now at the stage of being *consciously incompetent*. He's incompetent at something only now he *knows* there is something to be competent with.

The child practices, failing at first but eventually getting it until he becomes *consciously competent;* he can tie his shoes but has to concentrate in order to do so. After enough practice, it becomes second nature; he can do it without thinking about it. He has become *unconsciously competent.*

There are four steps to go from unconsciously incompetent to unconsciously competent.

1. Unconsciously Incompetent leads to →
2. Consciously Incompetent which leads to →
3. Consciously Competent which leads to →
4. Unconsciously Competent

Relationships are no different. Marriages begin by not knowing what it is that you don't know, what it is that you are missing to make the relationship successful. We may be hard-wired to seek out being part of a "We" but we do not know what it is or how to get there. We start out being *unconsciously incompetent*. The process of moving from an "I" to a "We" involves going from an unconscious marriage into a conscious one, getting to know and discover one another deeper and more securely as time goes on.

This is a process and frustrations are perfectly normal. The mystery of our mutual attraction, coupled with our childhood wounds and uncertainties isn't a perfect recipe for success. For the relationship to grow in a healthy manner, we need to increase our knowledge of one another, discover the questions we need to ask, and in that process create a safe haven for the relationship can grow.

An innocent remark may spark a tirade from your spouse. You have no idea what landmine you just stepped on. You may have just unwittingly said the exact same line her abusive father used when she was a child. You are unconsciously incompetent; you don't even know what the trigger was and your spouse may not either.

Working as a "We" requires you to recognize patterns that could keep you away. For instance, anger never brings people together. If you find a discussion getting heated, recognize the pattern and share that awareness.

FREEDOM TO LOVE

To be free to do something, you must be free *not* to do it. We are free to love only to the extent that we aren't forced into love by guilt, shame, fear of abandonment, or, worst of all, the interpretation of vulnerable feelings as emotional needs. No matter how seductive, "I need you," may sound in popular songs, the partner who needs you cannot freely love you.

If someone needs you, then he or she is more likely to abuse you than to give freely of love and support. Most painful conflicts in committed relationships begin with one partner making an emotional request, motivated by a perceived "need", that the other, motivated by a different "need," described as a demand. Any disagreement can feel like abuse when the perceived "need" of one party to be "validated" crashes headlong into the "need" of the other not to be manipulated.

The "need" becomes a weapon.

"If you loved me, you'd do what I want (or see the world the way I do)," one argues. "And if *you* loved me, you wouldn't try to control me," the other counters.

This is why surface-level communication and problem-solving techniques are not long-term solutions. As long as they perceive themselves to have emotional needs that their partners *must* gratify, their desire to love is reduced to, "Getting my needs met," which the partner often perceives as, "You have to give up who you are to meet my needs."

The Perception of "Emotional Need"

An emotional need is a preference or desire that you decided must be gratified to maintain emotional equilibrium. The sensation of need begins with an increase in emotional intensity; you feel more strongly about 'doing this' or 'having that.' As the intensity increases, it feels like you *need* to do or have it.

The perception of need falsely explains negative experience. If I feel bad in any way for any reason, it is because my needs aren't being met. It doesn't matter that I'm tired, not exercising, bored, ineffective at work, or stressed from the commute and the declining stock market; I feel bad because you are not doing what I want.

Once the mind becomes convinced that it needs something, pursuit of it can easily become obsessive, compulsive, or addictive and almost certainly self-reinforcing. Obsessing about the preference or object of desire increases emotional intensity and the perception of need; the more I think about what you should do for me, the stronger the perceived need grows. Failure to control one's behavior regarding the desired object has the same effect: continually criticizing you for not meeting my need increases the perception of need.

In terms of motivation, emotional needs are similar to addictions. While the body contributes to an addiction, the mind decides exclusively that you have an emotional need.

The Entitlement of Emotional Needs

Perceived emotional needs come with a sense of entitlement. I have a right to get you to do what I want because I need it, and my right is superior to your right *not* to do what I want. They also include a coercive element; that is, if you don't do what I want, you will be punished in some way, at least by withdrawal of affection.

Relationships driven by perceived emotional needs are likely to produce power struggles over who has to do what to meet whose needs. If you seek to get your needs met in a relationship, you will become as demanding and manipulative as a toddler, but, unlike a toddler, you're almost guaranteed to get depressed or chronically resentful.

Adults have Desires and Values

In contrast to perceived emotional needs, desires are positively motivated; if what you desire is based on your deeper values, the act of desire makes you a better person. For example, the desire to love makes you more lovable, i.e., more loving and compassionate.

Desire is appreciative, *not* entitled. If I desire something, I am more likely to feel appreciative of it than if I feel entitled to it. Much of the distress in relationships stems from the deterioration of desire into entitlement, which is what people mean by feeling "taken for granted." In contrast, relationships driven by desire and values engender a sense of meaning and purpose.

Ultimately, the freedom to love is a core value. Which is more important to you, getting your perceived needs met or loving freely?

PHILLIP & MARY: A CASE STUDY

Phillip P. and his wife Mary had been married for 11 years. Phillip came home one day with a surprise for his wife that he was ecstatic about. His 7 years of working extra hours and playing office politics was about to pay off.

He just got promoted at work.

He had asked his wife to take over their finances the week before. He walks in the door beaming with pride. He's carrying a box of filet mignon and a bottle of wine; ready to barbe-

cue it on the grill and toast to the celebration of his achievement. He was headed to the grill in the backyard excited about
Mary's reaction, when she looked up at him and asked, *"What's
in the bag?"*

He proudly stated, *"I got this promotion at work, so I bought
filet mignon and your favorite wine. We're going to celebrate!"*

Her eyes narrowed as she coldly asked, *"How much did that
cost?"*

He was puzzled and honestly didn't remember the exact cost.
He was too excited about his promotion to care. *"30 or 40 bucks
I thnk,"* he stated. To his answer of thirty to forty dollars, she
complained that it was too expensive, they could have burgers at
Costco for a lot less. She turned around and went back to set-
ting the table.

Phillip was more than deflated, he was ticked.

He had worked his butt off for this promotion and celebrat-
ing it with his family was his way of getting some recognition at
home.

He flipped out.

"Are you kidding me?" he shouts. *"What about that $90 perm
you got last week. I give you the checkbook and all of a sudden
your whining about some steak and wine? At least we both get to
enjoy this dinner."*

The argument went downhill from there.

He tells her how manipulated he feels by her and how no
matter what he did, he felt abused. She exploded with rants
about a past expenditure of his over 3 years ago for $200 that
prevented her from getting a gift for her mother. They were no
longer talking about the specifics. The celebration spiraled down

into a disaster. Mary then paused….she took a breath, lokked down and held up her hand.

"Just a second, honey…I think we got off on a tangent, here…. .you know…I…," she drifted off and began to cry.

She gives him a hug, looks up into his eyes and says, *"I'm really sorry."* She tried making a connection, but at this point he is so filled with anger and frustration, when she asks if he still feels that she's manipulating him, he says, *"Yes, it does."* At that point she withdraws and goes off into her room.

Did their conflict have anything to do with the filet, wine or a haircut?

No.

During our consultation, they both came to the same conclusion. He needed validation, admiration, and a few words for what a great job he did at work to earn the promotion. Her focus had been financial security. She was blind to his needs and she invalidated him outright.

Mary, on the other hand, had a need for security and to feel that she was doing a great job with the finances. Her need for certainty and a solid financial future was paramount. The expensive groceries & wine created a spike of uncertainty that made her feel disrespected. When her awareness kicked in and she leaned in to reconnect, she became vulnerable to him.

Had they *both* securely connected, Phillip would have been aware and recognized their mutual needs. However, he was still angry and therefore blocked from being self-aware. His "I" wasn't working. As a result, her olive branch of vulnerabilty did not create any trust or connection.

He was still unconsciously incompetent.

To avoid such confrontations like this in the future, Phillip and Mary used the tools we taught them at our WE³ workshops to instantly be aware of themselves and become unconsciously competent.

If you catch yourself in a similar situation, don't get stuck in the argument or in the heat of the moment. Think how and *why* you are truly feeling, analyze how and *why* your partner is truly feeling.

When Phillip and Mary shared this experience during one of our follow ups to the workshop, they shared a similar event that occurred just 2 months thereafter.

In this case, Mary had received an award from the no-kill shelter where she volunteers one day a week. She was very proud of this award as it is one of the rare "Lifetime Achievement" awards they ever give out. The day Mary got the award was the same day Phillip's biggest client left the firm; causing untold stress at his office.

"Honey, you'll never guess what happened at the shelter!" she beamed. Phillip's head was down and as he was about to make a rude, 'who cares' type of comment, still reeling from his awful day at work, but he paused and thought a moment. He recalled his thought process, *"I thought maybe I should look up and instead of being a smart ass, I would use this opportunity to snap out of my funk."*

He looked up at her and she was holding her award.

"I instantly connected with her positive energy and my mood changed instantly. She was beaming and I was so glad I looked up before commenting," he reflected.

They had securely connected and became unconsciously competent. Moving through these four stages isn't always permanent.

We all need reminders from time to time. Going from unconsciously incompetent to unconsciously competent takes some practice and a few triggers to help your awareness. Below are a few tidbits to help you get to this level and be a loving "We" again.

o Don't make someone feel powerless when you can empower her.

o Don't make them feel alone when you can connect with them.

o Don't make them feel uncertain when you can provide security and comfort.

o Don't take when you can contribute.

o Finally, don't walk away when you can walk towards one another.

Remember STOP, an acronym that best sums up the content of this chapter.

Suspend Judgment- about what you think is going on

Think- about what might *really* be at cause.

Observe- what the both of you are doing.

Process- what you see and find the real issue beneath it all.

Chapter Five Summary

- Get past denial, find out your partner's emotional needs
- Know what you don't know, become unconsciously competent in your relationship
- Freedom to love comes from unconditional love
- Recognize the patterns that keep you away.
- STOP: Suspend judgment, Think, Observe, Process

Chapter Six:

STEP 3:
COPING STRATEGIES

"Relationships remain an endlessly fascinating and often frustrating puzzle."

People have different ways of coping with their traumas, patterns they developed as children and continue to use into their adulthood and in their relationships with other people, including their spouse. Many of these coping styles revolve around our being an individual, an "I". As an empowered "We" you'll need s new tools or coping stategies to develop a secure, effortless and permanent connection.

Before you install "good" coping strategies, it'll be helpful to recognize old programming patterns that you have used in the past.

COMMON COPYING STYLES AND PATTERNS

The coping styles we all employ are initially developed in our childhood. These were used to deal with a past pain or trauma.

If you grew up with abusive parents, you may have become a frightened, passive victim or the rebellious defiant child that leaves home at an early age. The resultant coping mechanisms depends on the temperament we were born with and how unconsciously choose one parent over as a role model.

For instance, when an "Abuser" marries the "Victim"; the child might choose to copy one of those or a combination of the two. In either case, the coping style selected is used to survive childhood.

By the time we reach adulthood, our styles of coping become well ingrained into our psyche, and we repeat these styles long after survival needs as a child has passed. The responses don't disappear as they become part of our personality and communication style.

They become maladaptive responses.

These unconscious responses lead us to act in ways that block our development. Instead of growing and improving ourselves from our conflicts, many people become isolated, stubborn, or suppressive with our emotions.

All conflicts allow for three basic methods of coping.

Surrender: The surrenderer gives in to the situation and allows it to repeat over and over again. This person becomes submissive, avoids conflict, and is passive. They rely on others and constantly seeks affiliation. They become a people-pleasing follower.

Avoidance: The Avoider tries to find a way to escape or block the situation. Avoidance has subsets that can take several forms.

- Social Withdrawal: The person seeks social isolation and excessive autonomy. They often have an exaggerated insistence on self-reliance and independence over involving others. This person will sometimes retreat to private activities, such as too much television, reading, or surfing online.

- Addictive Withdrawal: Avoiding the world by withdrawing through drugs, alcohol and over eating.

- Psychological Withdrawal: This includes any form of psychological escape, including numbness, denial, fantasy, and other forms of dissociation.

Counter-Attack: The person who counter attacks does the opposite of what is being imposed upon them. Like the Avoider, counter attacks can take several forms.

- Aggression: The person counter-attacks by attacking and blaming others, being overly critical.

- Dominance: An excessive need to directly control others to accomplish one's goals.

- Manipulation: Any method of covertly exploiting others is deemed okay, be it dishonesty, seduction, or conning.

- Rebellion: On the outside they may appear compliant, but they are punishing others or covertly rebelling through procrastination, pouting or complaining.

- Excessive Orderliness: Insists on maintaining a strict order to the point of obsessiveness. Has excessive adherence to his routines and rituals, and devotes an inordinate amount of time to find the best way to accomplish his tasks while avoiding negative outcomes.

By reverting to theses coping styles, a couple in conflict turns away from one another; they have become subjects of their ingrained subconscious responses. Communication must be balanced and equal, turning towards one another instead of against.

Eye-rolling is not communication, neither is the "either-or" way of thinking that leads to such absolute responses as, "I'm right, you're wrong". Rely on your old coping strategies while in a conversation with your spouse and it *will* become a fight if it wasn't already. One might play his domineering strategy, forcing the other into the submissive role. Another might be trained from childhood to always be on the alert for a fight, and so as an adult seek them out, always be expecting a fight in anything their spouse says and react accordingly. Or you might resort to the blame-game.

Any of these sound familiar?

The different types of cycles and interactions are endless but all of them result from our old childhood coping strategies. Learn to adapt different coping strategies that allow you to *turn towards* one another, positive responses where the couples become masters of their relationships instead of its victims. Learn to work through your problems, thus forging a deeper connection, in even the most negative of situations.

Positive coping strategies, like becoming self aware, require understanding, tools and practice. Here are a few ideas that we use at our WE³ workshops.

HEAD SPACE VERSUS HEART SPACE

There are a large variety of responses that a couple can have to different situations. Sometimes it comes down to being preoccupied; too much in either their head or their heart to pay attention to the other person and connect.

Someone who is involved in an activity, be it watching television, doing a task, or working, is in his head space. Task-oriented people are often so preoccupied their brains don't even register that you spoke.

Coming out of this state would take some effort on their part and probably be seen as an interruption to his job just as surely as if you had walked into his office while he was in the middle of a conference. As a "We" you both have to gently find the right time and manner to move out of the head space before engaging in a discussion.

Someone in their heart space is able to connect emotionally with another about his fears, needs, dreams, and desires. However, being too much in your heart space may leave you unable to focus on anything except a specific issue, on an insignificant detail. A person who only has heart space may end up turning away instead of turning towards their partner. You become less interested in hearing what the other is saying and more interested in making them hear you about your one detail. The other becomes unimportant.

How many arguments have revolved around one spouse being fixated on one minor issue like it is the end of the world, while the confused partner is trying to draw attention to some more significant matters? It's like a computer program that is stuck in a loop, reprinting the same message over and over again on the screen. Nothing gets done, no progress is ever made.

Before you open up a proper communication channel with your spouse, make sure you are both in a balanced space between head and heart. Be sure you can *see* one another and hear what each is saying. Actively focus on the act of communicating before you begin, or you are just saying words.

The Emotion That Lies Beneath

Emotion in Latin means "to move", so emotions are going to move couples in different ways depending on which emotion is present. Identify which emotion lies underneath your partner's response in a conflict before attempting to resolve the conflict. Like the child that cries all the time; simply telling them to be quiet won't solve the underlying problem that caused them to cry in the first place. Rather, one should look beneath the surface for *what* is making him cry; then deal with that issue. The ability to connect one's outward actions with the underlying thoughts, feelings, and emotional states, is called "mindsight" by psychiatrist Daniel Siegel of UCLA, and is the basis for self-awareness and empathy. Strong emotional memories get chemically recorded in the brain and can later manifest in our actions from a trigger, unless we are mindful of them in ourselves and in others. Knowing the possible types of emotions that can lie beneath one's actions is an empowering first step towards understanding your partner.

Here are a few typical emotions that lie beneath what you may see on the surface.

Shame: You tried to create an emotional connection but there is a lack of authenticity or vulnerability because of some imperfection. Shame means hiding, creating emotional distance as a means of protecting one's self from fear of judgment or criticism. This is a big one with men.

Anger: This is usually an emotion of moving against. Be it passive-aggressive anger or hostility, you are trying to protect yourself because an alarm went off in your head shouting "Danger" about the current situation. Anger can be a healthy release, but it becomes unhealthy in a marriage when left unresolved and bitterness and hurt are allowed to linger.

There are two types of anger:

- The kind that creates passion or energy.
- The kind that results in destruction and hostility.

Healthy anger can get you to act for the good of the relationship, to protect yourself and the one you love. The unhealthy kind, however, places a wedge into a relationship. Unhealthy anger hurts the one you love when left unmanaged.

Joy: The emotion of joy is about the desire to connect and share something with another. A very positive type of connection, but if it is met with a negative, angry or dismissive response, joy can quickly evaporate.

Sadness: Sadness as an emotion learned from something we have seen or experienced. Sadness is asking to be comforted, to open a communication with someone who can relieve us of the pain of sadness. Seeking comfort, however, can make us dependent. Taken to the extreme, one can become functionally dependent upon another. We become so used to being dependent on our partner for relieving our sadness that it becomes habit. We end up avoiding responsibilities and dealing with the original problem that made us sad in the first place.

Any of these above emotions can make you dependent upon another, for the good or for the bad. Being dependent upon one another is not bad; in fact, it's at the core of any healthy relationship. But when one becomes dependent to an extreme, the imbalance becomes unhealthy. The dependent one begins to shirk his or her responsibilities. The dependency slides from a bonding mechanism to an obsession. The other partner begins to feel like they have a tumor growing on their back. The unhealthy dependecy becomes fuel for aggression.

A couple that is co-dependent upon one another, however, is a couple in balance, a couple in love. Their mutual dependency becomes a healthy coping mechanism. A healthy co-dependent couple is able to depend on each other for support, but if their partner is unavailable, they don't fall apart, as in the case of an unhealthy co-dependent relationship. As Steven Covey states in his book, *7 Habits of Highly Successful People*, the couple becomes inter-dependent.

Whatever the apparent reason for an argument or conflict in a relationship, look for the emotion that lies beneath. It's not about the checkbook or the steak you brought home, it's not about how uncaring he *seems* to be that his wife lost her baby, it's about what we don't tell one another, and it maybe something we've nearly forgotten about ourselves.

Coping With Good And Bad[8]

You come home after a great day and your partner treats you like something the dog left in the back yard, or you're pulling that cake out of the oven and it falls flat, ruining your kids birthday party. We tend to view things as either all good or all bad, then resolve the problem by keeping good separate from bad. This black and white view of a world of grays leads us to deny all the shades in between and an inability to tolerate weaknesses and failures in ourselves and in others. If we fail then we are bad, and if we succeed then we are good. By extension, we see everything our partner does in that same

---

[8] Henry Cloud, John Townsend, Boundaries, Changes that Heal

light and therein lies the circular reference that freezes the relationship like a computer.

There are four ways of dealing with the conflict between good and bad results, only one of which works.

Deny The Bad: Denying your faults, the denial of your emotions as not being acceptable, or denying the existence of sinful feelings such as lust or envy lead to sadness and an inability to cope with the problem that caused it. Nothing goes away.

Narcissists have this affliction. So focused are they on themselves, that they deny anything they do as being wrong, sinful, or unacceptable. This makes them unable to cope with relationship problems because they see no problem; at least not with themselves.

Deny The Good: Often one has become so buried beneath a pile of "ideal" expectations that they do away with standards altogether and live without any awareness of being bad. Alternately, we deny the good in others and view everyone as being all bad, always having ulterior motives, and no one caring for anybody but themselves.

You will often see this manifested in teens. So buried by expectations from one authority figure or another, they'll often say, "Screw it," and ignore everybody as not knowing anything as they pursue their own teen rebellion. If not dealt with or corrected by the time they reach full adulthood, they could slip into the alternate version where they view everyone as being bad and self-serving, including whomever they may decide to partner with.

Attack And Judge: This is the most common way of dealing with the bad. While there may be some truth in the attack, if it is not done with some grace and acceptance, the result is harsh and hurtful.

A harsh attack and judgment from one partner upon another can often lead to the other partner responding in kind with his own attack, and that only spirals out of control. Alternately, the one attacked could retreat. This accomplishes nothing but engendering bad feelings and another problem added into the mix. It is a fine line you walk if this method is used to cope with conflict; a misstep in either direction away from constructive criticism could be viewed as an attack.

Acceptance: Here we deny nothing, accept both the good and the bad as parts of Life. The bad can be forgiven, while the good is our idealized goal. We meet both with grace and acceptance. We deal with both as they show up in our lives. Since we do not condemn, detached acceptance allows us to love and connect with the other.

Acceptance, naturally, is the only way of dealing with the conflict between good and bad. This style of coping works 100% of the time. It will always lead to communication and results that both sides can accept and leave plenty of room for love to continue to flourish.

BUILDING THE BRIDGE THROUGH TALKING[9]

In addition to acceptance, let's examine some great tools and ideas to build a strong "We" beginning with the art of conversation. Each conversation you have deposits more coins into your love bank. However, knowing know *how* to talk, requires one to understand your partners *love language.*

---

[9] Love Language, Gary Chapman and Sharon Morris-May

Love language is about knowing what your partner means when they says something. Let's take the example of the hard working couple, both working full time in careers, raising a family and success oriented. A common excuse for their relational conflict is not having the time to unwind and talk. She used to like going for take-out on Friday nights but he insists she cook a meal on Fridays. She says she's exhausted and that he's too demanding. But from his point of view it's not about the meal or even how it tastes, it's about showing him she is contributing and pulling her own weight. He cooks the other four weeknights, and he just wants to see her contribute that one night. What she had taken as simple complaining was something else, but she could not see that until she had figured out how to speak his language in the way that he meant it.

Blah, blah, blah…

Relational gridlock results from simple miscommunication and your marital computer has now frozen. It could have been the wrong choice of words, or quite often, simply the tone. You may have meant your tone as nothing more than being too tired to smile, but your partner will take it to mean you are being mean and belligerent. Start by backing away from your automated responses and begin to analyze what your partner is saying. Take a sincere, hard look at what *you* are saying and the way you are saying it. Don't assume your partner is telepathic. Be clear and upfront.

Start be actively listening.

Listen to the *way* in which something is said. When it's your turn to respond, keep it light. If you are responding emotionally, it may sound too critical and defensive. This style of commuincation is an open invitation of the Four Horsemen into your conversation. Speak from a place of feeling, not aggression. Keep it conversational. Break the tension from time to time with a little humor if that is your way. Remember you're both on the same side.

There is such a thing as intentional versus non-intentional conversation. Non-intentional is casual conversation, the topics won't have any serious impact on anyone's lives. Intentional conversation, on the other hand, is an expectation to be listened to and is best exemplified by the old, "Say what you mean and mean what you say" axiom. A real close conversation with your partner, the kind where you connect with that person thoroughly, should always be intentional. Have an atmosphere where each person talks openly and honestly about his or her conviction, is unafraid to voice any concerns or beliefs, but does so in a manner that precludes any hostility on either's part.

Be focused. Be present.

Next, be empathetic towards one another; do not assume the worst in what he or she says. Always give each other the benefit of the doubt. He might have had a bad day and his words came out wrong, or she may have simply been too tired and worn out to phrase things better. Remember what you know regarding your partner's personality type. If you both have strong personalities, then remember to tone it down. She is still your beautiful tenderhearted wife and you are still the one she sees break out into childish grins under the right circumstances.

It's been said we are given two ears and one mouth and they are best used in proportion. When it is your turn to talk be sure you thoroughly understand your partner's point. If you don't, ask a few clarifying questions, first. When they realize you were actively listening, they will be more receptive to your point of view. Help them understand what is important to you about the issue and why. When you ask clarifying questions, nod your head and pause before responding, you are *actively listening*. Active listening means you don't simply hear the other's words, but you understand it from their point of view. Show an interest in what is being said; be a part of what the other is trying to tell you. Don't interrupt, don't judge, and don't start trying to think of counter-arguments; this is not a debate class. You may not agree with everything said, but you can give the courtesy of actively listening and validating your partner's value, if if you disagree with their point of view.

So to summarize, here are our four steps to better communication:

1) Make sure that you are clear and understood
2) Watch the *Way* you say something
3) Be empathetic to whom you are conversing.
4) Listen to what the other is saying.

Everyone wants to be heard, understood, and validated. It shows caring. Once you have each communicated your side of the issue to one another, it may be time to find middle ground. What solution can you find that you will both be happy with? Compromising is about finding that middle ground, but too often people will use the word "compromise" as a means to trick the one person into conceding to their demands while getting nothing in return. Do not distort the concept of a compromise but stay true to its spirit and find that middle ground.

Don't just communicate when you *have* to, and don't assume that she knows that you love her. People like hearing affirmations on a regular basis. A quick kiss in the morning, note on the pillow, message texted at lunch, even a quick phone call from work just to say, "Hey, I love you, you know." It's not always about the words but about hearing the tone. If you hear that loving tone from one another on an often enough basis then when a crisis comes up you will both be in a better place to deal with it, talk it out, and remain close during the entire process.

Successful couples invest about 20 to 30 minutes a day reconnecting, talking about their needs, what happened that day, what they're looking forward to, etc. Beyond that, we should also invest another ten to fifteen **hours** a week of quality time together. You rarely have to offer solutions for your partner's problems, in many cases, being heard is validating enough.

To better learn your partner's love language:

- Listen
- Understand
- Validate

From Joe:

"I'd like to say something to her without her freaking out."

Why's her reaction a problem? What's wrong with your partner freaking out?

Most folks have shared with me the reason they hold back their truth in a relationship is because their partner can't handle it or will get too upset. Sorry folks, but the main reason many of us hold back is that we are afraid. Afraid of what? For most people, they are afraid of our reaction to their reaction. We are afraid of our own stuff that gets triggered when they get triggered. This is the enmeshed stance in a relationship. "I can't be me because I might upset you, so I'll protect myself and withhold what I really want to say." Meanwhile I rob them of the opportunity to grow by not saying anything. So what if the other person gets upset? That is their problem, not yours (and, if we are on it, we can make space for their reactivity and love them through it). We have to learn how to be smarter and more courageous than this in a relationship, especially if we care about being who we truly are, and especially if we really do love the other person. Let's give them a chance and trust they can handle who we are.

CURIOSITY

Curiosity is the difference between merely wanting to hang out with someone else but not really care where you are, and being motivated to know more about that person and what makes him tick. This is the first step you took when courting your spouse or partner.

Flash forward a few years and what don't you know? Her favorite music used to turn you on. Now it's a mundane conversation about the 80's. You used to be fascinated by his business travels, now you've been to so many places, you don't even get excited about your next trip.

How can we keep our excited, curious natures thriving if we 'know' everything about our partners?

Everyone changes over time, depending on what goals they have reached and on the experiences they have had. What changes them inside? What new experiences have shaped their opinions? What were your dreams fifteen years ago and what are they now? What cereal did you like then and which one now? Maybe after fifteen years she got sick of chocolate covered raisins only you didn't realize that and so thought she was trying to insult you by refusing them. Don't assume; get curious.

Even if you can finish each other's sentences, you cannot know how they may have changed over the years unless you keep in communication. The mystery will always be there, ever changing and evolving. If you don't stay in communication, you will start to feel detached.

She was a stranger when you first courted, so court her again.

Get curious enough to know who she or he has become over the years. Don't make assumptions based on what you *used* to know about your partner, don't feed the frustration with ignorance or apathy. That is a solid road to disconnection.

If you aren't sure where to start or even how, there is a powerful technique called Mind Mapping, or for our specific relational subset, Love Mapping.

Mind Mapping (Love Mapping)[10]

What is a love map? John Gottman, author of *The Relationship Cure*, descibes the love map as the part of your brain where you store important information about your spouse. It's a mental notebook where you store unique traits of your spouse. It includes your spouse's dreams, goals, joys, fears, likes, dislikes, frustrations, and worries. Your husband's favorite breakfast cereal or the name of your wife's best friend are important "points" on the map.

Unfortunately, most of our internal love maps keep us a bit lost. Without properly organizing a "legend" and a visual connection of your fears, joys, etc. our internal love maps remain a mystery to most. Why are thorough love maps so important?

---

[10] John Gottman, The Relationship Cure

When you have a clear picture of one another's love maps, it strengthen's a relationship. Couples with clear love maps remember important dates and events, and they are aware of their partner's changing needs. They constantly seek updates on what the other person is doing, feeling, and thinking. Being known in this way is a gift each partner gives the other, bringing great happiness and satisfaction. It also helps couples be better prepared to cope with marital conflict.

In one study Gottman interviewed couples around the time of the birth of their first child. For 67% of couples this stressful event was accompanied by a significant drop in marital satisfaction. The other 33% did not see such a drop, and many felt their marriages improved. The difference was the completeness of the couples' love maps. "The couples whose marriages thrived after the birth had detailed love maps from the get-go. . . ," says Gottman. "These love maps protected their marriages in the wake of this dramatic upheaval."

Couples who established a habit of finding out about each other's thoughts and feelings were likely to continue doing so at a time of change. Their deep knowledge about each other and their practice of staying in touch protected their relationships from being thrown off course. We have a blast creating love maps in our WE[3] workshops. They are fun, interactive and get created in a very playful manner. While we cannot re-create this experience in this book, you can start by creating your love map by asking each other some questions:

Family: Which of my parents do I think I'm most like? Why?

Friends: Name two of my best friends and how I met them.

Work: How do I feel about my boss? What would I change about my job?

Hobbies: What are my three favorite things to do in my spare time?

Dreams: What is one of my unrealized dreams?

Favorites: What is my favorite dessert? TV show? Sports team?

Feelings: What makes me feel stressed? When do I feel confident?

Answer these questions about your spouse:

1. He/she's sitting in front of the TV, what is on the screen?

2. You're out to eat, what kind of dressing does he/she get on his salad?

3. What's one food he/she doesn't like?

4. You go out to eat what kind of drink would he/she have?

5. Where did he/she go to high school?

6. What size shoe does he/she wear?

7. If he/she was to collect anything, what would it be?

8. What is his/her favorite type of sandwich?

9. What would this person eat every day if he/she could?

10. What is his favorite cereal?

11. What would s/he never wear?

12. What is his/her favorite sports team?

13. Who did he/she vote for? The one who actually had experience.

14. Who is his/her best friend?

15. What is something you do that he/she wishes you wouldn't do?

16. What is his/her heritage?

17. You bake him/her a cake for his/her birthday.

18. Did he/she play sports in high school?

19. What could he/she spend hours doing?

From Savannah:

There was one couple that used mind mapping to find out where their problem were in their sex life. They would watch separate televisions at night. He would access porn while she would be watching a late night talk show. In therapy, she became uncomfortable with how explicit he was about his sexual fantasies. It was an uncomfortable experience for her, but she finally listened to what he was saying.

As it turns out, his fantasy was MILF porn. I simply pointed out that his wife is also the mother of his children, and rather good-looking, which makes her a MILF. It was an epiphany for them both. His eyes widened as he realized, "My wife IS a MILF," and he suddenly looked at her like he wanted to devour her, while she was thunderstruck with the thought, "Oh my God, I'm a MILF." Suddenly their relationship was aligned in a direction they hadn't explored before.

Regardless of your challenge, mind mapping can be a great coping tool. Love maps are so important, in fact, that all participants at our exclusive WE³ retreats get a customized set of maps. The WE³ program is best summed up by what "E³" stands for: Experimental, Empowering, and Entertaining. The program includes interactive conversations and dialogues, an examination of the couple's attachment styles, and practical applications of what we have been talking about in this book, the neuroscience behind it, and what it means to really be a "WE". The payoff of the seminar is a couple dancing to the same beat and step across that dance floor of life.

The transformation we deliver is permanent.

Your Best Moments Are Together

Pop quiz.

Who is your best friend, the person who you want to spend the most time with, your closest fan and entertainment, the one you want to do nearly everything with? If you had to pause before answering, "My spouse," then a little examination is in order.

Time to get a new best friend.

"But, I have my best friend Nancy! We go shopping all the time and have a blast!" You can still keep and go shopping with your friends, but your best friend should be your mate.

You may not want to go shopping with your spouse, and she may not want to watch the big game with you. Your partner will most likely not fulfill all of your needs. However, your core needs for connection should be with your primary relationship.

What will you be doing 5, 10, or 15 years from now? What are your goals? Not just your individual goals, but your goals as a couple. Is it paying off the mortgage? Is it opening up a business? Or maybe a special trip on your tenth anniversary. Find something to get excited about and celebrate any mutual milestones for the both of you. Get your partner invovled with your personal dreams and ambitions. The more you share your personal vision, the more likely your partner will share theirs and you can find commonality between the two.

You shared your stress from work, your failures and hard times, right? So share your good times, share your pie in the sky dreams, share the joys. This is more than just "hanging out" together; it is planning a future, looking forward to the realization of a common ambition. You are each such a huge part of the life of the other; having goals together is critically important. Keep one another updated on your daily wins and losses, celebrate each other's victories, but plan as well for ones you will be able to celebrate together.

Relationships are built upon the stuff of dreams and fantasies, so don't be afraid to keep dreaming. Keep sharing your personal dreams to fuel your dreams as a couple.

Just as it is important to share victories, it is equally important to be there for one another during times of crisis. Fighting alone is a lonely battle indeed, but having your partner there for you can make all the difference in winning that battle. Keep your communication channels with one another clear, any critiquing of each other non-offensive, and you won't have to worry about being hurt by your spouse, but be able to stand together with confidence against whatever assails you.

Remember, your best friend is your spouse. Friends share respect, enjoy spending time with one another, and make you feel good to be around. You may not always share the same opinions about everything, but you don't work against one another either. You share your past good times and work to create some more, and you are always there for one another. That is friendship, and the one to whom you are drawn as a spouse or partner should be your closest friend of all.

CASE STUDY

Barbara and Jim W. were, by all appearances, a successful couple. They had financial stability, great careers and were respected in their socail circles as a "perfect couple."

Behind closed doors, they were emotionally dying.

During our work with them, we discovered a disconnect when it came to discussing each other's dreams, fears and desires. Even after having been together for twenty years, they felt almost like strangers. They have kids who are nearly adults, she has pre-menopausal and he was becoming more and more distant. Barbara started developing symptoms of anxiety and some claustrophobia. Much of this was a result of hormonal shifts, some of it beneath her own awareness. She had a hard time asking for her needs to be met. For Jim, this "new Barbara" was overwhelming. According to his love map he didn't have a clear idea of what was happening and had not been curious enough or interested in these changes and how it affected the "We" in their relationship.

The situation became galvanized in a moment.

Barbara had a frozen shoulder for a couple of years. She had an MRI and possible surgery scheduled. Her anxiety was at an all time high. Jim was considering scheduling an out of town meeting just to avoid her anxious behavior!

Fortunately, with the help of the love map, he learned to become more aware of Barbara's needs. Instead of avoiding the potential conflict, Jim tuned into her anxious discussion about her upcoming MRI and he asks what time it's at so he can clear his schedule. He knows she has claustrophobia, and the enclosed MRI will definitely increase her anxiety.

Before the appointment, Jim asks the doctor if he can be in the room with her. The doctor agrees, and now as the MRI is cycling through and she looks to be having a panic attack. Jim firmly grabs her leg just to let her know that he is there. She immediately calms down and the MRI proceeds.

When it was finished, she had surprised herself. The only fear she'd had was not the enclosed MRI, but was that Jim would let go. He had been there for her, forged that connection, and through the simple act of holding onto her leg found a way of coping with her claustrophobia and the MRI scan. Barbara and Jim W. were always admired as a couple for their outwardly connectedness. Privately, it became more true than ever.

Something as simple touch can create a secure connection.

It is through securely connecting that a relationship is not just re-booted, but upgraded with intelligent and loving software.

Chapter Six Summary

- Common Coping Styles: Surrender, Avoidance (social withdrawal, addictive withdrawal, psychological withdrawal), Counter-Attack (aggression, dominance, manipulation, rebellion, excessive orderliness).
- Know the difference between Head Space & Heart Space.
- Four Ways of dealing with the conflict between good and bad: Deny the Bad, Deny the Good, Attack and Judge, Acceptance (the only one that works)
- Learn your partner's Love Language.
- For Good Communication: Clearly communicate your needs, be empathetic, never assume the worst, give your partner time to talk and *actively* listen, don't just communicate when you *have* to.
- Get curious about what the other's current life, likes, and dislikes.
- Mind Mapping is a simple yet powerful tool to discover the sexual and emotional problems between you and your spouse.
- Your spouse/partner should also be your best friend.

Chapter Seven:

BRINGING IT ALL TOGETHER

"Thoughts become actions. Actions become habits. Habits forge permanent change."

Life is lived through our relationships; with our friends, our loved ones, and our children. Unfortunately, social isolation has become a pandemic in America, with twice as many people being socially isolated today as compared to twenty years ago. The more stress Life has to offer us, the more we need a confidant, a loved one that will be there to support us when times are troubled and cheer us on during times of joy. Someone whose very support will, in turn, give us the confidence in ourselves that we need to move on and live a great life.

You found the *one* person in all the world that wants to connect with you, be a part of your life and be in love with you. By getting to the end of this book, you have shown your desire to reboot your relationship.

Even if you don't feel that way now, you once did.

Pause, reflect and open your mind to the possibility that your connection can not only rekindle, but become stronger. It doesn't matter if you are feeling a bit awkward or have already filed divorce papers. Your relationship can not simply reboot, it can flourish.

It's funny that the things that are most valuable in life are things that cannot be purchased with money, invested, saved or stored. The things we truly value can only grow when they are given away.

Our hearts, our vulnerabilities and our love.

Your primary relationship is not simply the lightning rod for your heart. If there are children around, they will emulate how you cope, how you talk and how you act.

What should you do now?

EVERY NIGHT IS FOLLOWED BY DAY

There is indeed *hope,* that the two of you can manage against whatever assails you. Like the computer with the glitch in the software that needs a technician to fix it, we are the expert love technicians that can help you fix the glitches in your relationship. We can help you *reboot* your relationship.

Let us conclude with another story. Antonio and Ginny A. were a couple who came to us with problems both financial and cultural. Ginny was Dutch. As therapists we are taught that the Dutch culture are not a highly connected culture. They are a little bit smoother and less emotionally available than a Hispanic person would be.

Antonio was from Nicaragua, and was a highly paid well-known musician when they first met. Five years later, in his early 40s, they had a baby and Antonio decided he wanted to spend some time connecting with his family. Ginny felt somewhat emotionally disconnected to begin with. With Antonio's hietus, she finds increasingly out of the loop as she increases her work hours to maintain their lifestyle.

Bringing in more money now than her husband, she treats him as an inferior, which, as a Hispanic male he naturally has issues with. Because of his upbringing and attachment style, strangely enough, Antonio is not programmed to say, "You know what? I'm still man of this family and I really want to set the course for how we're moving ahead through this challenging time." He was vocal to others, but not to Ginny.

He needed some exercises to help him regain his title as man of the family, so we put him on a three-step program.

1) Set goals

2) Watch his communication style

3) Find quality time

The first step we told him to take was to set goals. Plan a date night, which he had not. Plan for birthdays, vacations, and holidays. You can't be in charge of your family and its activities if you don't take charge.

The second step was about communication style. It takes one person to start a fight but two people to continue it. Watch out for signs of the Four Horsemen; criticism, defensiveness, stonewalling, and contempt. The minute Antonio saw any of those creep into his conversation he'd call a time out. He did this consistently for 3 weeks.

The next thing he needed to do was work in quality time. As mentioned, successful couples schedule ten to fifteen hours a week together. That's the goal, though at this early stage in their reconnection I would be ecstatic if they worked in at least *two* hours.

To get him to become self-aware, I asked him, *"How do you treat your mother when you visit her? Do you throw down your bag and go straight into your room?"*

Of course not. They sit, talk, smile, and laugh; they bond and connect, are not dismissive of one another. So why, then, is he not that way with his spouse? By buying into his spouse's state, he is just as guilty as she is for their problems. If he wants to be man of the house then he needs to step up and fill that role. Don't expect to be perfect the first time you input a change. Begin by setting the ground rules of how you want things to be.

When we first meet our partner, there is no rulebook on what to look out for; we just do what we can with what we're given. With this text the hope is to show you how to correct your relationship, know the signs of when things have gone too far, and how to make things better than it ever was once you get past your own ego.

Ginny, Dutch wife, needed to work with how she connects with other people, even though she didn't feel she needed to change. How are her ten emotional needs being fulfilled in her life? How are other people showing up for her? She'd had a previous marriage with two kids but has no contact with them, and whenever they do get together she is unable to connect with them emotionally. This is a cultural issue that goes back to what her parents had done, but she needs to dig deep and see how happy she is with that situation. Only when she realizes that she is not happy with something will she then decide to make a change.

Ginny and Antonio were on the verge of filing for divorce. Their counseling lasted only a few weeks and one month after attending our WE3 workshop, we heard they were planning on having another baby. I asked her about their feelings on this, *"Oh, Antonio is as happy as a lark. At first, I was a bit nervous, but we are getting along so much better, we felt it would be a great addition to the family."*

There are no guarantees in life, but one thing I am confident of is Ginny and Antonio's ability to navigate their differences use the correct coping mechanisms to stay a securely connected couple.

How does one realize change is desired?

For each of the key relationships in your life, describe them in detail. Find the positive things that happened in those relationships. For Ginny, we asked her to tell me how it felt when her sons were born. She then described every other incident related to that feeling in detail. Reflect and connect with the feeling insidd of you when your spouse proposed, when your son hit that home run, when your wife had that surprise romantic dinner waiting for you at home "just because", or when you both bought that house *together*.

After you've categorized your milestones, look at what happened to those relationships. Where are they now? What improved? What dissolved and how did you cope? What manner of pain was left in its place? People change for two reasons:

1. Fear of loss, or

2. Hope of regaining.

In this example, the instigator for change will be her fear of losing her connection with her husband, even if she does not yet realize it. Just remember to:

1) Find the positive in what was.
2) Examine the resultant fall-out.

RELATIONSHIP SOLUTIONS[11]

Imagine having a partner that was so passionate towards you that every time you walked through a door you felt like it was first-love all over again, tingling from head to foot. Then when you're flying around on a business trip, landing in another state, the first thought in your head is not about the business but being in your husband's arms. For Ginny's entire life, that feeling of connection was completely foreign to her...even with her children.

It was only through their mutual discovery of themselves and dedication to the "We" that Ginny and Antonio turned their journey completely around. When they came to us, there was talk of separation and divorce. As of this writing, their marriage is as vibrant as when they were dating.

In order to uncover your coping strategies and install better ones, take a look at what may be happening in your current situation. Are there hurtful exchanges and habits that don't serve the "We?"

We've covered a huge amount of ground in this book and hope you can attend one of our WE3 workshops. If you ever get caught in a conversation or situation that stops you dead in your tracks, reflect on these seven basic principles of empowered relationships. Master these and you may find the rest of your problems falling away.

---

[11]Willard Harvey, Love Busters

Seven Basic Principles

Trust:

All relationships are ultimately based on trust. To build trust you must simply keep your word, remain consistent, and be dependable in everything you say and do. Never say or do anything that can shake the trust the other put in you.

Respect:

Take the time to deliberately express your respect for what makes your partner unique, valuable, and important. Don't expect your partner will automatically know that you still share that respect.

Communication:

The amount of time you take to invest in communication with your partner increases the value of the relationship. Listen attentively, calmly, and quietly, and give him or her your total attention, and they will return the favor. Show respect for one another in the way you converse.

Courtesy:

Saying "please" and "thank-you" on a regular basis will make them feel better about themselves and raise their self-esteem. This is especially important with people we care about the most.

Caring:

The greatest gift you can give one another is unconditional love and acceptance. Never condemn, criticize or complain.

Look for ways to show that you care for that person, make them feel respected and loved.

Praise and Appreciation:
When you express your appreciation for something another person does, they feel better about it and will do more of it. The more you give, the more you'll get. This is true of smiles, appreciation and gratitude.

Helpfulness:
The seventh principle for success in a relationship is to be helpful with those people whom you live with. Being willing to step in and assist with the little burdens.

When you take a moment each day and apply these seven simple principles to your relationship, you'll fend off the darker clouds heralded by the Four Horsemen. It is far easier to take the time to check the oil of your classic car on a regular basis than to wait until the entire engine needs replacing.

Your Action Plan

If you don't qualify for a WE³ retreat, then there are still a few things you can do to restore the love you once had for one another. A quick little step-by-step that can go a long way.

Step 1: Commit to Moving Towards.
Before you can understand each other's needs, become self-aware and execute all the steps to creating secure attachments, you have to commit to the process. Don't go after rebooting

your relationship with a "let's try and see what happens" attitude. Commit to proactive solutions.

Step 2: Understand the problem.

Becoming self-aware isn't easy and it rarely happens in an instant. By consistently using the tools in this bok and applying them on a daily basis, you'll not only become a better person, but you'll likely create a more approachable person within your partner. Understanding is freedom.

Step 3: Create a plan.

Discuss things open and honestly, then create a plan that will work. Don't judge. Don't attach emotion or feelings to the outcome or words. When you work as a team on what you both want, the synergy of the "We" comes to life. Follow the road to reconnecting on the dance floor of Life.

Step 4: Look at the emotional needs.

There is a significant amount of discussion regarding emotional needs because we begin our love through emotion. Identify which emotional needs have to be met, then work towards fulfilling those needs using the communication techniques and coping styles that are empowering to the both of you.

IT IS IMPOSSIBLE TO HAVE A BAD RELATIONSHIP IF SOMEONE IS MEETING ALL YOUR NEEDS.

If you can't meet your challenges it is because you are not really committed to the plan, not committed to change. You may feel like it's your partner's fault alone and not your own, and in some cases maybe it is.

However, since it is impossible to change another person, your only canvas is your own. Your only influence on your partner is how well you improve your "I".

HOPE

We start out as two "I's" seeking to become a "We." It is in the seeking that rests a powerful drug of recovery.

Hope.

Hope is not a wish, not something in the future, but comes from four areas in our lives:

➢ Character

➢ Experience

➢ Wisdom

➢ Strategies

Character allows us to hold our hope against any odds. A person with resolve is said to be of good character. Experience develops our character, so new experiences give us new hope. And finally, there is an old proverb that tells us that wisdom and insight give us hope. How so? With the experience and wisdom, we can develop a strategy, a path to our solution, which in turn gives us hope.

Hope is a vital ingredient in any relationship, for without hope there is no reason to work towards something greater.

We go into relationships without mastery; completely unaware and lacking in experience. Ther is no manual to teach us the ropes, give us the wisdom and insight we could use to forge an eternal bond.

Hope is born from these four siblings of virtue, all of them together not just one or two. If you are playing baseball for the first time, the first time you see that ball coming at you at a hundred miles an hour looking like lightning wrapped in leather, you have no way of understanding what to do and just might dive to the ground to avoid getting hit. But practice a hundred times and you begin to understand, your hope grows that you will be able to hit that thing when you step up to bat. You have gained the experience and wisdom, developed methods to handle it and gained insight from that, then finally have the character to bravely stand upon that mound and take a swing at it. You have hope that you will hit it. Professional players have even more experience and that ball doesn't seem like it's coming at you nearly as fast anymore, the chances of hitting it far greater. Your hope has grown into a knowing that, "Yeah, I got this."

You don't have to buy it, but you do have to invest in it authentically and consistently. Where you were once disconnected and isolated, hope will be a spark that you can fan the flames of communication, connection and love to enjoy your life.

Hope is free.

REBOOTING YOUR RELATIONSHIP

Love is not about demanding that the other meet your demands, but freely and unconditionally meeting the other person's needs. It is a mutual exchange of love and acceptance that no amount of strife can ever long get in the way of. Glitches may develop, like in a computer program, but may be fixed and, like the ailing computer, the relationship rebooted to continue in its optimal operating state.

You have the tools, the assistance, the desire. Get back on that dance floor and float across it with your partner. The smile on your face may not be immediately recognizable, but it is authentically yours because you took the time and energy to love openly, live honestly, communicate non-judgementally and connect securely.

Congratulations.

You have rebooted your relationship.

Chapter Seven Summary

- Relationship Repair: Set goals, work on communication style, reserve 10-15 hours of quality time per week
- Rediscover the positive things in your relationships, then imagine the pain of their loss if you fail to change and reconnect.
- Realize that a problem exists
- Uncover the old coping strategies you have been using that have not been working. Change them.
- The 7 basic principles of a relationship: Trust, Respect, communication, courtesy, Praise/appreciation, helpfulness
- Your action Plan: commit to it, understand the problem, create a plan, look at the emotional needs.
- It is impossible to have a bad relationship if someone is meeting all your needs.
- Hope grows from: Character, Experience, Wisdom, and Insight
- When you have Hope, you can fix *any* relationship.

Appendix:
The Relationship Society

About The Relationship Society

Social psychologists and researchers have pointed out that, over the last 100 years, the American culture's fabric has been losing massive ground around what they call "social capital." Meaning as a people we are more isolated, alienated, and alone as people and have lost our core "human connection." This isolation has become traumatic to our well-being, as demonstrated by the millions in the United States suffering from chronic anxiety and depression, divorces surging, and less people marrying because of this ongoing phenomena. People are turning away from churches, synagogues, and a healthy community, and are turning towards internet-based relationships, making of every man an island unto himself.

To provide real answers and solutions to such a significant problem, this program was launched and is designed to build a collective mindshare, create connecting moments and experiences, and connect people to the human touch and contact through these programs. As part of the Relationship Society Initiative we will be introducing new programs and services to our community that will truly transform relationships and family life through connections and belonging.

The WE³ Couple Restoration Retreat

Throughout this book we have mentioned our WE³ program. The retreat program is designed to engage couples in a 3-day experience to powerfully impact and fortify marriages by teaching skills to go from good to great, or from a lack of love to rediscovering their love. The retreat is a three-day, 18-hour marriage boot camp that promises to radically improve marital dynamics in communication and intimacy by focusing on creating transformation and life.

Problem Statement

Couples don't have proper support, training, and know-how to manage their marriage. Marriages today face a mountain of challenges, with busy schedules, family-of-origin issues, work expectations, addictive behaviors, affairs, and dwindling romance all conspiring against healthy marriages. Often the mountain of marital problems seems insurmountable, prompting too many couples to give up and consider divorce as their best option.

Consider this sobering data: Sixty-seven percent of younger Americans agree that "when parents divorce, children are more prone to develop serious emotional problems." Marriage in our culture has weakened, the divorce rate doubling since the 60's. In a recent study of divorcees, the majority wished they had tried harder to salvage their marriage. Before making any life changing decisions, consider this: is there another way to escape the tragedy of divorce and recover hope for your marriage?

Although the U.S. divorce rate is at its lowest since the early 70s, the business of divorce in the U.S. is an increasing $28 billion-a-year industry. Ironically, in spite of the escalating financial costs of divorce, many families are finding that money is, by far, the cheapest price they are paying for it.

It would be hard today to find an adult who doesn't have some idea of the hard costs associated with divorce, but most agree that legal representation is both a necessary and expensive part of getting divorced. Understandably, with attorney fees ranging from $75 to $450 an hour along with up-front retainers of $500 to $10,000, a divorce these days comes with a pretty high price tag. Along with attorney fees, there are court costs for filing, process serving, mediation, subpoenas, and even more should your case go to trial. It is estimated that the average cost is $20,000, and when a divorcing couple has children other costs are involved, including financial determinations for child support and alimony, all of which have significant financial ramifications.

According to research done at John Hopkins University through the National Institute on Aging, divorce can also leave long-lasting effects on mental and physical health that remarriage might not repair. They found that divorced people have 20% more chronic health conditions such as heart disease, diabetes, and cancer, than married people do. The same study found a 23% increase in divorced people having mobility limitations, such as trouble climbing stairs or walking a block. For years, research has shown that being married increases life expectancy but now we have research that indicates the quality of life for married people is increased as well.

While it's nearly impossible to calculate the exact costs of divorce, anyone who has been involved in a divorce knows that it undermines and devalues everything that gives us a sense of security, significance, and well-being in our lives.

For this reason, the Relationship Society believes couples can survive and overcome whatever suffering, conflict, or hurt their marriage has experienced. The WE³ Intensive is proven to turn even the most hurting or devastated marriages into thriving and committed ones.

Project Intentions

The Relationship Society provides counseling, seminars, and workshops to help individuals, couples, and families resolve conflict in a healthy positive manner, manage stress and anger, address troubling emotional issues, restore and strengthen damaged relationships, and discover and realize their dreams and potential. This includes supportive services to help the disadvantaged as well as intervention, recovery, and prevention programs addressing substance abuse and domestic violence affecting women and children.

Goal #1: *Education and Training.* To increase a couple's emotional connection, develop relationship skill building, and teach techniques. We will not only educate couples based on the best practices and finest materials available in the marriage counseling field today, but also on what has been proven to work. We base our marital training on results.

Goal #2: *Empowering* married couples means more than giving them relationship competency and knowledge. The key is to teach them how to take effective action upon what they have learned.

Goal #3: *Entertain.* In today's world, most people want to be entertained while being educated. This program capitalizes on this fact, and engages them on an intellectual and emotional level. Secondly, when couples are being entertained, they become more emotionally engaged in the dynamic process of change that energizes from within and between, and are more likely to retain and act on what they have learned. To carry out this part of the program, video clips, music, and other experiential exercises will be employed.

Goal #4: *Creating a safety net* and sense of community so no couple falls through the cracks.

The three-day WE³ Intensive is designed for one couple and two couple coaches or counselors and/or a small group of 12-20 with two highly trained and qualified marriage coaches.

The WE³ is 92% successful in keeping couples together and increasing satisfaction in their marriage. Couples are given new strategies and tools and given time to implement them with coaching before leaving. Emotional communication, problem-solving, and conflict resolution are addressed.

THE PROGRAM

Here is a quick run-down of the WE³ program and the Seven Transforming Conversations of the Zen, also known as the "Velvet Sledgehammer." If you are interested in attending the program, please contact us for arrangements.

(I) Recognizing Dragon Conversations: In this first conversation, couples identify negative and destructive remarks in order to get to the root of the problem and figure out what each other is really trying to say. Dragons are our past experiences that trigger negative reactions and the cycle. Trauma is both outside/externalized (Ellis) and within the cycle, enemy of the dance.

(I) Finding the Trauma, Raw Spots, Vulnerabilities: Here, each partner learns to look beyond immediate, impulsive reactions to figure out what raw spots are being hit. Frame emotions and cycle in terms of: a couple's search for connection and the unhelpful ways of managing or mismanaging the disconnection. I frame this as a "Fight for Connection." These are ways they attempt to get their partner to understand, respond, and care that actually hurts and drives their partner away, leading into the cycle or vortex.

(We) Revisiting the Vortex: This conversation provides a platform for de-escalating conflict and repairing rifts in a relationship and building emotional safety, and identifying the cycle of the trauma, need/fear dilemma, etc..

(We) Connecting and Getting to the Heart of the Matter: The heart of the program, this conversation moves partners into being more accessible, emotionally responsive, and deeply engaged with each other.

(We) Forgiving Injuries: Injuries may be forgiven but they never disappear. Instead, they need to become integrated into couples' conversations as demonstrations of renewal and connection. Knowing how to find and offer forgiveness empowers couples to strengthen their bond.

The WE^2 and WE^3 system consolidate all of the above into a congruent program of:

(We) Aliveness, Power, Freedom, Self-Expression, Authenticity Consolidation, Integrity & Intimacy: This last conversation is built on the understanding that love is a continual process of losing and finding emotional connection; it asks couples to be deliberate and mindful about maintaining connection. Even though there is conflict, one must stay connected through the conflict.

As an added bonus for this book, in the next three pages we have included a worksheet for couples to use to help them work through their need/fear dilemma, or the "vortex" as we call it. As you can see from the above, we delve into the vortex a lot more as part of the Program, but this should get you started. Credit for "The DNA of Relationships for Couples" worksheet goes to Greg and Gary Smalley.

REFERENCES

To better assist you in reconnecting and finding one another in the jungle of Life's strife, here are some books that might also help you out, as well as the web site where you can have your relationship checked out, and how to contact me personally.

Online Relationship Assessment:
The Couple Checkup $29.95
www.couplecheckup.com

ABOUT SAVANNAH ELLIS – INFIDELITY COACH & RELATIONSHIP SOCIETY, COO

Savannah Ellis has coached thousands of couples and individuals from Sydney, Australia to Las Vegas, USA to help them achieve their relationship and personal goals. Her passion is to help people be authentic to themselves and others.

Savannah specializes in infidelity counseling and personal empowerment; having personally coached many cases specifically helping couples survive and recover from relationship infidelity. She provides specialized coaching and seminars to move people through hard times and onto an easier path.

Savannah provides coaching, training and consulting programs to conscious large corporations and small business owners who want to educate their people on what workplace affairs can do to individuals professionally as well as personally.

After working for corporate giants such as IBM & AC Neilson, she knew she could capitalize on these skills for motivating people and creating change. Savannah is a serial entrepreneur, and has founded her own businesses including: Mineral Makeup wholesale and exporter, Promotions & Events Company; Beauty Product Importing & Distribution, Beauty & Hair College, Bars, Nght clubs, Day spas, Salons, Medical Offices, Accountancy & Bookkeeping firms. She,Äôs a certified Business Coach, and Keynote speaker, training with ICON International in 2002, and growing a business coaching practice from 0 to 450 clients in only 1 year, requiring 20 full time employees.

Savannah holds Psychology degrees from Monash University, Australia: Bachelor Behavioral Science (BBSc), and post graduate degrees in Clinical Psychology. She also has many years of business management and coaching experience, and holds Management qualifications: Master Business Administration (MBA) and a Doctor Business Administration (DBA). She is currently completing a Masters in Mental Health Counseling through Walden University, USA.

Savannah is a member of the Australian Psychological Association (APA), an Associate Fellow Member of the Australian Institute of Management (AFAIM), and a Certified Prepare & Enrich Facilitator . Savannah is featured on Cheaterville.com, & DearPeggy.com

1070 W. Horizon Ridge, Suite 200
Henderson, NV 89012
415-877-4004
relationshipsociety@gmail.com

About Joe Whitcomb –
CEO, The Relationship Society, Licensed Psychotherapist, Relationship Coach, Educator, and Author

Joe Whitcomb, CEO of The Relationship Society, brings more than 20 years of relevant experience to his work as a relationship coach and therapist. With a focus on helping couples connect and communicate at deeper levels, Joe provides effective tools for putting the fun and excitement back into relationships using his proven multidisciplinary approach. Joe earned a B.S. in Psychology with an emphasis in Neuroscience and BS in Organizational Management from the University of Maryland College Park. He holds a M.A. in Clinical Psychology and Marriage and Family Therapy and Masters in Business Administration from Pepperdine University and a Doctoral Candidate in Psychology and Marriage and Family Therapy from The Chicago School of Professional Psychology. Joe's understanding of the complex nuances presented in modern relationships make him a respected expert on personal development and interpersonal relationships.

Building on his belief that everyone is entitled to the power and freedom that come from a healthy relationship, Joe delivers a customized program filled with techniques that couples can use for the rest of their lives. By combining his formal education with his real world experiences, Joe guides couples through his signature WE³ process which is experiential, empowering, and entertaining. Expanding beyond traditional methods, Joe assists clients facing a variety of challenges including infidelity, communication blocks, blended families, empty nest syndrome, and more. Couples work with Joe to honestly assess their relationship and learn new behaviors and techniques for relating to each other.

After helping more than 2,000 couples navigate their relationship challenges, Joe wanted to find a way to support even more people who want to experience the joy of authentic, loving relationships. His vision came alive when he created The Relationship Society, a progressive community designed to address the loss of social capital and relational connectedness in today's society. As a safe space for successful individuals to find relationship strategies and resources, The Relationship Society is a premier collective of subject matter experts and thought leaders assisting members with their personal and relational growth. The Relationship Society's flagship seminars include the WE^2 and WE^3 programs which are multiple day intensives for couples who want to experience more intimacy and address any challenges in their relationships. Couples consistently report enjoying more intimacy and better communication after experiencing these events.

Joe is a member of the American Association of Marriage and Family Therapists, International Honor Society of Psychology (Psi Chi), and licensed as a marriage and family therapist in California.

A lifelong learner and lover of adventure, Joe enjoys spending time with his children and granddaughter and also finds time for sky diving, dancing, and cycling.

Connection is why we're here...
Life is about relationships...
Health is Social...
Joe Whitcomb, M.A. LMFT
Licensed Marriage and Family Therapist MFC 51093
Doctoral Candidate
CEO/Founder
The Relationship Society
2730 Wilshire Blvd, Suite 650
Santa Monica, CA 90403
310-560-0726
www.relationshipsociety.com
www.facebook.com/therelationshipsociety.com
jwhitcomb@paznaz.org

3700 E. Sierra Madre Blvd, Counseling Office
First Church of the Nazarene (PAZNAZ)
Pasadena, CA 91107
310-560-0726

6593070R10111

Made in the USA
San Bernardino, CA
11 December 2013